ESCAPING
TOXIC
GUILT

*Five Proven Steps to Free Yourself
from Guilt for Good!*

SUSAN CARRELL, R.N.

Mc
Graw
Hill

New York Chicago San Francisco Lisbon London Madrid Mexico City
Milan New Delhi San Juan Seoul Singapore Sydney Toronto

Library of Congress Cataloging-in-Publication Data

Carrell, Susan.
    Escaping toxic guilt / Susan Carrell.
        p.   cm.
    ISBN-13: 978-0-07-149735-0 (alk. paper)
    1. Guilt.   I. Title.

    BF575.G8C36   2008
    152.4'4—dc22   2007025785

1 2 3 4 5 6 7 8 9 10 11 12 13 14 15 16 17 18 19 20 FGR/FGR   0 9 8 7

ISBN   978-0-07-149735-0
MHID   0-07-149735-8

McGraw-Hill books are available at special quantity discounts to use as premiums and sales promotions, or for use in corporate training programs. For more information, please write to the Director of Special Sales, Professional Publishing, McGraw-Hill, Two Penn Plaza, New York, NY 10121-2298. Or contact your local bookstore.

This book is printed on acid-free paper.

Contents

Preface

I don't travel much, but I've been on a guilt trip since I can remember. My life reads like a travelogue of guilt. I hate to think about the psychic fuel I've burned worrying whether I've let someone down. The carsick queasiness of feeling I've not been good enough, or careful enough, or just *enough* is all too familiar. Preoccupation with what will so-and-so think has a nauseating roll to it as well.

I stayed home when my children were small and felt guilty for not using my education and contributing to society. When I went back to work, I felt guilty because I couldn't be there for my kids. I hung out six years too long in a bad marriage to a drug-abusing physician. Why? Too guilty to leave—after all, he needed me.

I institutionalized the rest of my care-taking tendencies: First I became a registered nurse and devoted myself to caring for people in psychiatric hospitals and treatment centers. My own good emotional health and fortunate circumstances compared to those in my care gave me an unremitting case of guilt—I owed, *I owed*. Then I became an Episcopal chaplain. I felt chronically guilty in that position—can a minister ever give or do enough? In my early days as a Licensed Professional Counselor, I cringed with guilt every time a client didn't grow and blossom as I expected he or she should. So I know guilt intimately.

In my work as a therapist and relationship coach, I've seen myself in the lives of many of my clients. They are people who try their best to do the right thing, compassionate individuals who respect the feelings of others, rule-following folk, responsible citizens—good people whose life journey has been complicated, compromised, or completely derailed by guilt.

Folks on perpetual guilt trips seem more vulnerable to the wretched emotion than others. It's as if some personality types are born to be overly giving and feel guilty when they fall the least bit short of their own high standards. In many ways they are prisoners of guilt, trapped by good intentions, perfectionism, an inflated sense of responsibility, and misinterpretations of religious expectations.

Flawed beliefs learned from family systems, societal precepts, and religious heritage are the underlying culprits. What if it *isn't* so noble to organize your life around other people's needs? What if it's possible for you to be a good person *without* taking care of every needy soul who passes your way? And what if you're *wrong* about what you think God expects of you? I have explored beliefs learned from family, society, and religion that I once took as bedrock, and I have discovered that they often fall short because they are simplistic answers to complex problems.

The powerfully dark side of guilt can trap a man or woman in a miserable marriage, enslave the parents of an errant child, and keep a person from claiming his or her sexual identity. My desire is to bring hope and liberation to good people who struggle with difficult life situations in which guilt is winning over reason, good judgment, and faith.

I think a story is the best teacher, and so most of the ideas and concepts presented are illustrated through storytelling. A mental health professional is a story collector, and I have been collecting people's stories for over twenty years. All the stories used are real stories of real people. I have carefully disguised the identities of my clients by altering certain facts such as name, occupation, age, or gender and on occasion have combined the stories of two or more clients with similar features. I also share my own stories and hope they lend credibility and sincerity to the work.

You will find self-score quizzes in many chapters. These are not scientifically constructed examinations but are meant to be guides to help you decide if guilt is behind your trouble. Although it is possible that if you answer yes to even one question guilt could be the culprit, I have placed an arbitrary number of yes responses in each quiz to offer a reasonable prediction of guilt. I hope the quizzes stimulate your thinking and help you uncover guilt if it is there.

Acknowledgments

It takes a village to write a book, and I have a village of people to thank—but I will narrow the list to the main contributors. First and foremost I thank my clients for allowing me to participate in their lives. It is an honor to work with people who courageously search below the surface to find their true identity and live into it with determination. I am grateful for my agent, Regina Ryan, who was willing to take on a rookie and is the best coach ever. I am thankful for my editor, John Aherne, who understood me and was able to bring out the best of what I have to offer. I was lucky enough to have found Carol Conway, my freelance editor who helped me craft the first draft into a workable document. I am indebted to my dear friends and colleagues, Maggie Megalynn and Paula Caplan, who were always encouraging, generous with their time, and let me pick their brains at will. Last but not least, I am blessed to have Winston, my true companion, who listened to my ideas, kept me from losing sight of the mission, tolerated the time lost to us, and supported me with unwavering affection.

Introduction

A Hidden Net

Are you marooned in a marriage that is not affirming and joy-ful? Do you feel trapped in a dead-end relationship? Do you have a valued friend who sucks the life out of you? Is your life dictated by your needy and demanding children? Are you stuck in a job that you hate? Does the need to please your parents rob you of healthy independence? Does keeping in-laws happy cause con-flict between you and your spouse? Are you unable to claim your sexuality? Are you unintentionally pregnant and unable to make important decisions about what to do?

If any of these situations describe your life, this book will help. Being trapped in a painful relationship or distressing situation is a miserable state of affairs. It's like being shipwrecked in a whirlpool. You thrash about frantically just to keep your head above water while you go 'round and 'round.

In my sixteen years as a licensed counselor and relationship coach, I have worked with many good people who suffer need-lessly because they are caught in a powerful current that renders them helpless. I am able to help my clients break free because I know and understand the force behind their struggle. It's a force they often don't recognize. It is a force that is powerful, pervasive, and can affect every single aspect of their lives. The name of this powerful force? Guilt.

Maybe you already understand that guilt is the problem but find you are powerless to overcome your feelings. On the other hand, maybe all you know right now is that you are trapped in a distressing situation, and you can't break free and move on. You ask yourself again and again: why can't I do this?

You may have racked your brain, talked to friends, and read a book or two in a concerted effort to figure out why you can't do something to straighten out your life. You think that if you could only figure out what is holding you back, you could begin to change things. But if guilt is behind your immobility—and there is a very good chance it is—you might not be able to recognize it.

Guilt is tricky and delights in disguise; it is subtle and insidious. Guilt is also one of the deepest and darkest emotions in the human condition. Even if guilt doesn't play the leading role in your troubles, it's very likely that it is involved in your situation to some degree.

Some people are more prone to the ravages of guilt than others. If you are reading this, chances are you are vulnerable to guilt. You quickly and easily feel guilty about all sorts of things. You are a "good person" who tries to make the world a better place, a "responsible person" who holds yourself accountable for your actions. Others see you as dependable and reliable. But although you work hard to have good relationships, deep down you may feel powerless because you know that others have more power over you than they should. Maybe you frequently feel used. When I talk about feeling trapped, you know exactly what I mean.

To begin the process of breaking free and escaping guilt, you need to find out if it is holding you prisoner. If you already know that guilt is the culprit, you're ahead of the game, but you will benefit from additional understanding of the trouble the emotion can cause and from new ways to think about it.

I am not interested in changing your basic personality, and you shouldn't be either. You are probably like many guilt-ridden people—sensitive about and responsive to the needs of others. If that describes you, then you have a quality that is valued and needed on this planet and that you should value in yourself. What we want to do is hone this basic ability into a way of being in the world that is good for both you and others. I'll be your coach in this adventure, and as with any good coach, my job is to help you bring out the best in yourself. An athlete has innate strength and aptitude, as do you; my goal is to strengthen the abilities you already have and help you develop new skills so you can play the game of life in the most effective way possible.

In order to overcome the power of guilt, it is important to understand the nature of the emotion. Part I provides that knowledge by examining the key characteristics of guilt and explaining some of its most important psychological and cultural underpinnings. This is followed by a look at the types of people who seem to be experts at making others feel guilty. Part II explores the eight most common guilt-inducing situations.

Once you figure out why you feel guilty, and which kind of person is most likely to make you feel guilty, it's time to do something about it. Over the years, I developed some key strategies for helping people move beyond their guilty feelings. In Part III, I will teach you to break free from guilt in a step-by-step process that you can apply in any guilt-laden situation. Here is an outline of the five steps.

- **Step One: Speak the Truth.** In Chapter 15, I will take you through the first step and help you see how important it is to be truthful with yourself about what is really holding you back. You must be able to identify and acknowledge the real problem of guilt. Maybe your situation makes you so anxious that your thoughts rush around too frantically for you to stop and analyze what is really going on. You feel you are working as hard as you can to make things better, but you don't seem to be getting anywhere.

It's as if you're on a bicycle. You pedal hard and you pedal fast; when it's clear you're not getting very far you pedal harder and faster. You sweat and pant. Surely you're almost to the top. But then you look up and realize you're on a stationary bike, struggling for all you're worth but not moving forward at all. After working through Step One, progress will be possible because you'll be able to recognize what's keeping you locked in place. Step Two tells you what to do about it.

- **Step Two: Claim Territory.** Step Two, presented in Chapter 16, is the key step toward escaping toxic guilt. It's about claiming your basic rights as a human being. You probably do a great job of respecting the rights and needs of others, but you have to realize that you have rights and needs too. You have the right to own and protect your own emotional territory, without feeling guilty about it. I'll teach you about the concept of emotional boundaries, and help you understand what's happened to yours. I'll also teach you how to reach inside yourself to access what's already there: the ability to repair, reclaim, and restore your boundaries without guilt.

- **Step Three: Brace for the Storm.** Step Three in Chapter 17 prepares you for the inevitable consequences that will occur when you begin to change your behavior to break the cycle of toxic guilt. Some people in your life won't like it. This step will be a challenge if you've spent your life accommodating everyone else. I'll give you plenty of real-life stories to help bolster your courage as you get ready for the onslaught.

- **Step Four: Ride the Wind.** Step Four, outlined in Chapter 18, may be the most difficult because it's about finally letting go of those past behaviors and patterns. Although you expected the storm and braced for it, it will inevitably cause some damage. It's not always possible to repair the breaks in relationships that occur when you change your behavior to become less accommodating and less easily manipulated by guilt than you once were. Guilt-ridden people are usually "fixer" types. When there's even a bit of friction between you and another, you rush to make it all go away.

You may find it is very difficult to release your grip on a relationship or event. You will want to manipulate the outcome so that everything comes out on a positive note. Relinquishing control can be a daunting task, but the end result is liberating. I'll show you that letting go and riding the wind, instead of trying to direct it, is freedom itself.

• **Step Five: Patrol Borders.** As you'll see in Chapter 19, you will be at risk for repeating patterns of behavior that are much older than the new steps you've learned. Step Five will teach you how to protect your emotional property and maintain your boundaries as time goes by so that you won't succumb to your old habits.

You will come to know these five steps well and be able to put them into play when you feel yourself falling into old guilty patterns and habits. If you are serious, really serious, about moving forward, plan to work hard to get out of your comfort zone and really challenge and stretch yourself with these five steps. The struggle will come as you choose to see things differently and do things differently. As they say in twelve-step recovery programs: if you always do what you've always done you'll always get what you always got.

Doing something new is both exciting and frightening. It's exciting to think that things can be different, that you can break free, and it's frightening to change the way you've always seen things and done things.

When we learn something new, we feel stronger and better about ourselves. Remember when you first learned to ride a bike, or swim, or spell five new words? You were proud of yourself, right? You'll feel that way again as you work through the five steps. And you won't be on your own: I'll be coaching you every step of the way. I'll give you encouragement and pointers as we go, and when it's time you'll be ready. The strategy is simple and straightforward;

best of all, it works. Although you won't become guilt-free, you will be able to manage your guilty feelings instead of allowing your guilty feelings to manage you.

I'll be encouraging you in every way, but only *you* can change yourself, and we human beings fervently resist change—even when we want it. You will have to be intentional and proactive.

So if you are tired of feeling trapped and controlled by others, and are ready to break free from the hold of guilt, read on. We have work to do!

Part I

The Guilt Trap

1

What Is Guilt?

Guilt is the emotion we experience when we feel we have done something wrong. It is the gnawing sense that we have done something we should not have done, or have not done something we should have done. It is the nagging awareness that we do not measure up, that almost everyone else can do it better than we can. Guilt is behind the fear that we are never quite good enough. When we feel guilty, we blame ourselves for what we think are our inadequacies. Guilt makes it impossible to feel content and at peace with ourselves.

Sigmund Freud, believed by many to be the "father of psychology," explained guilt with his construct of the psyche. He thought that the self is a delicate balance between states of mind called the id, the ego, and the superego. The id is the primitive, animal part of us that is intent on getting what it wants. It is demanding and self-centered, like a child. The ego is the rational and reasonable part of the psyche and functions like an adult. The superego is exacting and judgmental and would like to dominate the self, much like a parent. The ego (the adult) is the mediator between the id (which wants its way) and the superego (which wants to be in charge). Freud believed that guilt was the result of an overactive superego: the parent in us who judges us harshly and condemns us.

Whether Freud's idea was correct or not, it is a helpful model to use in understanding guilt. Many of us are very aware of a critical parental voice that lives in our minds and scolds us at will.

The Two Different Kinds of Guilt

Although guilt doesn't get much good press anywhere, and it won't from me, it is important to understand that not all guilt is bad. Guilt can be a negative energy that diminishes your life, or a positive force for change in your life. It is essential that you learn to recognize the difference between good and bad guilt.

"Good" guilt plays a crucial role in our lives, ensuring that we monitor the rightness and wrongness of what we do—an essential element of civilized conduct. Most of us feel guilty when we think we have done something wrong; that feeling pressures us to change our behavior for the better.

Unfortunately, there are people who have little or no guilt and do not feel bad about what they do. They have no sense of having committed a wrong. Since they have no remorse about their bad behavior, they do not stop. These are the people who think the rules were made for everyone else. At best, they are the ones who are basically out for themselves and don't much care who they step on along the way. At worst, they are the ones who commit heinous crimes against others.

Thankfully, most of us do experience positive guilt and find that it serves us well. Guilt can enhance our relationships with others. If you realize that something you did or said hurt your friend's feelings, you feel guilty about it and take action to make amends. Guilt can improve our relationship with ourselves as well. When you reconcile with your friend, you have a sense of doing the right thing, and that makes you feel better about yourself.

Guilt can be an asset in life, but it has a dark side. Excessive guilt diminishes our ability to enjoy many aspects of life, and it can cast a gloomy shadow on our relationships with others. If your mother makes you feel guilty every time you call her, you'll end up resenting her sooner or later.

But excessive guilt does the most damage to our relationship with ourselves. Since guilt makes you feel like you've done something wrong, you don't like yourself much if you feel guilty at the drop of a hat. How could you, if you feel as if you are constantly making mistakes?

Some people, and you may be one of them, live with such pervasive feelings of guilt that they have a sense of being deeply flawed. They feel that no matter what they do, they are never good enough. This feeling can become so overwhelming that emotional health is compromised and the ability to experience peace, contentment, harmony, and joy is lost. If something goes wrong in their lives or in the lives of those they care about, these people feel it is somehow their fault, even when it has nothing to do with anything they did or did not do. They may also believe it's their responsibility to fix it. These unreasonable condemnations and expectations are the consequence of inappropriate guilt.

Positive, or healthy, guilt has its own tell-tale characteristics, as does negative, or unhealthy, guilt. In general, healthy guilt motivates behavior that nourishes relationships and builds a positive self-concept, while unhealthy guilt makes you feel powerless over others and is not self-affirming. The guilt that motivates you to visit your ninety-year-old aunt in the nursing home from time to time serves both you and your aunt well. Your aunt is nurtured by your companionship, and you can feel good about yourself for doing the right thing. On the other hand, if you feel too guilty to leave town for the weekend because your aunt is in the nursing home, unhealthy guilt may have a grip on you.

When Guilt Is Healthy

Healthy guilt motivates us to do a number of positive things. It moves us beyond preoccupation with ourselves and our problems.

Society converts good guilt into mores, codes of conduct, and laws. Without these standards, the health and safety of the population is not secure.

The following are the characteristics of healthy guilt:

• **Healthy guilt encourages us to consider the needs of others.** Let's say you're having a perfectly delightful time reading in front of the fireplace, when the phone rings. You check the caller I.D. and see it's your friend who's going through a divorce. You'd like to ignore the call and go back to your reading, but you know that your friend needs to talk. A wave of guilt causes you to put your book aside and pick up the phone.

• **Healthy guilt can lead to acts of compassion or courage.** If you hear a sermon or read a newspaper article that causes you to see how wealthy you are compared to others in the world, you may be motivated to do something about the healthy guilt you feel, such as donating money or volunteering at a local shelter. Healthy guilt can also lead to acts of courage. If passing by a car wreck that happened right in front of you would make you feel guilty, you will probably stop and try to help.

• **Healthy guilt encourages honesty, loyalty, and fidelity.** Let's assume you're married and attend a conference in a distant city. While there, you meet an attractive, smart individual in your small group. At the end of the day, you suggest the two of you have dinner together at the hotel. Although you thoroughly enjoy yourself during dinner, you would feel really guilty if you lingered in the bar having drinks (and no telling what else) with the person later, so you excuse yourself, go back to your room, and call your spouse.

• **Healthy guilt helps us take responsibility for our actions.** You might not want to tell your boss you lost an important document, but when you see someone else being blamed, you feel guilty—and so you admit that you were the one at fault.

• **Healthy guilt encourages restraint and can help delay gratification when necessary.** You may desperately want a new car, boat, or computer, but you feel too guilty to spend the money because you have committed to putting it in your child's college fund. Along the same lines, you might like to play golf today—the weather is perfect and it's supposed to rain tomorrow. But you promised to watch the kids so your wife could go shopping with a girlfriend. After a few minutes of devising creative alternatives, you feel guilty and decide to stick to the plan.

• **Healthy guilt promotes self-respect.** If you allow someone to take advantage of you and use you, eventually you will feel guilty because you know you are not valuing yourself. You will probably demand a change or leave the relationship in order to restore your self-respect. On the other hand, if you feel guilty because you are not living up to your potential, you may be motivated to go back to school, get a better job, or sign up for volunteer work.

When Guilt Is Unhealthy

As you might have been able to tell by the title of this book, I like to think of unhealthy guilt as toxic. A toxic substance is poisonous, noxious, and sometimes lethal. Toxic guilt, somewhat like cancer, is healthy guilt gone awry. Just as cancer develops when normal cells morph into invasive, destructive cells that multiply excessively and interfere with physiological function, toxic guilt develops when good guilt grows out of control and interferes with healthy psychological functions.

The following are the characteristics of toxic guilt:

• **Toxic guilt makes us feel responsible when we are not.** Do you constantly worry about your spouse's happiness and become anxious and upset if he or she is quiet, preoccupied, or grumpy? Do you monitor the emotional state of your teenagers and feel you must do something if they are out of sorts? Although you simply cannot be responsible for anyone else's happiness, toxic guilt will make you feel that you are.

• **Toxic guilt makes victims feel responsible when they are not.** It seems obvious that a person who was sexually abused as a child has been the victim of a crime. However, most adult survivors of childhood sexual abuse inherit a heavy dose of toxic guilt. They feel guilty because they think the abuse was somehow their fault. They feel they must have been bad or done something wrong. They live with the notion that they are somehow dirty, unclean, marked, unholy, or worse.

• **Toxic guilt can cause us to endlessly give and become a "suffering hero."** If you spend your life taking care of everyone else's needs, might it be partially because you're looking for praise or recognition for your sacrifice? Stop and think about the various things you've heard people say that support the notion that sacrifice is a virtue. "Bob is a saint! He puts up with everything his bitch of a wife dishes out." "Judy couldn't wait to retire so she could do all the things she never had time to do, but when her daughter asked her to keep the kids so she wouldn't have to take them to daycare, Judy agreed. Now there's a fantastic grandmother!"

Comments like these underscore the idea that suffering is the mark of goodness or greatness. Toxic guilt can lead us into a tender trap: if I don't accept these miserable conditions, I'm not a good person; but if I do, I'll somehow be rewarded.

• **Toxic guilt twists the truth and blinds us to the reality of the situation.** If the thought of leaving your spouse makes you sick with guilt, you might make excuses for your partner even if living with him is hellish. You might think, "My poor husband has trouble keeping a job because nobody understands him. No wonder he's in a bad mood all the time." This would be a distortion if the real reason your husband loses jobs is because he is so difficult that nobody wants to deal with him, or that he is an alcoholic who desperately needs help.

- **Toxic guilt enslaves its victims.** If you are stuck in a love-less marriage or a dead-end relationship because you're too guilty to leave, then guilt has trapped you. If your children run your life because you feel too guilty to tell them no, then you are a hostage. If the need to please your parents robs you of doing what you want to do with your life, then you are a prisoner. Just think of what your life could be if you could disengage and be free at last.

- **Toxic guilt makes us doubt ourselves.** You may know what you need to do to make your life better (move, cut the purse strings with your adult child, come out of the closet), but if you are infected with unhealthy guilt, you will question yourself and lose the conviction of your beliefs.

- **Toxic guilt can cause us to abdicate responsibilities.** If you are a supervisor who gives positive performance reviews to your work team—even when they are not justified—because you want their approval, toxic guilt is at work. Similarly, toxic guilt is the culprit if you do not discipline your children when they need it because you are afraid they won't like you.

- **Toxic guilt causes us to blame ourselves for everything.** If you are determined to believe that you are responsible for every unfortunate event that occurs in your life, you have toxic guilt. It will make you believe that when there is trouble in your relation-ship, it is all your fault. Toxic guilt will convince you that if you were a better parent, your child would be more successful. It is the nagging sense that if you had been a more dutiful child, your mother would not be ill.

- **Toxic guilt makes us feel like we have to do it all.** Toxic guilt can make you feel like you have to do it all in order to feel like you are good enough. If you agree to serve on the board of your neighborhood association when you are already depleted by other obligations, toxic guilt has a grip on you.

These are just a few tools to help you distinguish between healthy guilt and unhealthy guilt. When you are faced with that all-too-familiar feeling of guilt, it would be a good idea to reread this chapter to help discern whether the guilt you are feeling can be considered good or toxic. Knowing that will help you guide your actions.

Now that we have some tools to help us identify good guilt and bad guilt, let's take a close look at ourselves and see what role guilt plays in our own lives.

2

Naming Our Guilt

When you are in pain, either physical or emotional, it's important to know what's causing it. Once you know the source of your discomfort, you can organize your thoughts and formulate a course of action.

Diagnosing Guilt

If you've ever had a physical illness with symptoms that you couldn't make sense of, you know how disturbing it can be. If your doctor couldn't make sense of them either, that's even more upsetting. Most people are relieved to get a diagnosis, even when their worst fears are realized. It is a relief to know that the pain isn't all in your head, that there's a legitimate physical cause for it. And it's comforting to know you're not alone, that others have experienced the same thing. Once you know what you're up against, you can learn about it and take responsibility for improving your condition to the best of your ability.

Naming the source of emotional pain brings the same sense of relief. You feel better if you know and can name the cause of your anguish. Here's why: when you can name what you are feeling, you can formulate a way to be in charge of it. When you cannot name what you are feeling, the feeling is in charge of you.

Padima's Story

Let me give you an example. I had a client named Padima who was the office manager of a large legal firm. Her boss told her to see a therapist because her "attitude" had been noticed by the firm's partners and coworkers alike. He accused her of having been generally unpleasant, curt, and even hostile over the past several months. Her job was on the line.

When I saw Padima for the first time, she was both defensive and frightened. "I'm not a hostile person!" she assured me. "The office personnel are too sensitive." Tears in her eyes, she lamented, "What can I do? My job is at risk."

Over the next few weeks the real story unfolded. My client was in the middle of legal action against her ex-spouse. He owed her thousands of dollars in back child support, and she was going after it. Initially, I assumed that her anger at her ex-husband was spilling over into the workplace. That was indeed a part of the puzzle, but it was not the key piece. My client didn't even suspect that guilt played a part in her anger, but in just a few weeks, we discovered that it had the leading role. It wasn't anger at her ex-husband that was causing her problems at work, it was guilt. She was feeling so guilty for taking legal action against the father of her children that she had become an emotional basket case. She thought of herself as a mean and vengeful woman—the bitch ex-wife who was trying to ruin the poor guy. This self-image was so disturbing that it made her touchy and short-tempered in the office. Although she couldn't see it, guilt was behind her "attitude" at work.

As soon as Padima identified guilt as the problem and understood how irrational her guilty feelings were, she stopped loathing herself. Feeling at peace with her decision to prosecute her ex-husband for failing to take responsibility for supporting their children, and confident that she was a good person after all, my client became less irritable at her workplace and everywhere else.

Why Is Guilt So Hard to Recognize?

Let's talk about why guilt is so hard to recognize, and then we'll see if guilt is the cause of your pain. If you don't know whether or not guilt is behind your suffering, it's not because you lack intelligence or insight—guilt can be very hard to identify.

One reason you may not be able to identify your own guilty feelings is that you can't see them. Human beings are experts not only at hiding things from others, but also at hiding things from ourselves. We place uncomfortable thoughts and feelings beyond the vision of our mind's eye. We don't want to see ourselves in a bad light, so we bury painful images of ourselves. We can do this both consciously and unconsciously.

Here's an example of how we do this consciously. When Jon discovered his wife, Sonja, was having an affair with their financial advisor, he was angry, hurt, and humiliated, but he did not want the marriage to end. Sonja was remorseful and wanted to save the marriage as well, so the couple decided to try marital therapy.

Initially, Jon was cold, accusatory, and critical of Sonja in sessions; he blamed her for everything. This is not an unusual stance for a betrayed partner, and I allowed Jon to express his feelings. However, after several sessions it was time to change course. I asked Sonja and Jon to each make a list of their part in the betrayal. Jon was aghast. He reminded me in no uncertain terms that Sonja was the one who had broken the marriage vows, not him. He was angry with me and accused me of "blaming the victim."

I asked him why he thought that Sonja might have been vulnerable to the attentions of another. He had no idea. He had been a good provider and a dutiful, loving husband, he said: what more did she want? Now it was Sonja's turn to be shocked. "How can you say that?" she asked, wonder and disbelief stamped in her wide-eyed stare. "You've been married to your work, not me, for years, and you know it!"

Slowly but surely Jon came clean. He had been feeling guilty for his lack of attention to Sonja for a long time, but he never did anything about it. His culpability was too hard to face. Jon was aware that blaming his wife for the affair made him feel less guilty about his own behavior in the marriage.

Here's a similar example of how this happens unconsciously. Tracy was married with two young children and was having an affair with her college professor. She was very much in love with the professor, who was single, and came to therapy to decide whether or not to leave her marriage. In session after session she detailed how adoring, attentive, and romantic the professor was in comparison to her inattentive, boring husband.

Then she called one day before her regularly scheduled session, desperate to see me. She had discovered the professor was involved with two other women. "How could I have been so blind?" she lamented. "As I look back, I can see there were all kinds of red flags, but I ignored them!"

After the affair blew up in her face, the fog lifted and Tracy's vision became clear. Tracy's husband was a good man and a good husband, and she felt terribly guilty for cheating on him and lying about it every day. The professor, a known womanizer, had never been as enamored with Tracy as she wanted to believe he was. The only way she could justify her behavior was to create an image of her lover as the ideal, adoring man. The image she created for herself was a fantasy. In other words, she wasn't lying about the relationship to me or to herself; she simply could not see the truth because it painted her in such a negative light.

It is not all that difficult to hide feelings of guilt from ourselves. I did it myself. I was a single mother when my kids were in high school. I was also in graduate school at the time and holding down a job. As a result, I could seldom attend my son's athletic events or my daughter's dance team performances. Instead, I became an expert at criticizing the stay-at-home mothers who were so much more involved in their children's lives. *Overinvolved*, I called them. *Intrusive*, I said. *These women don't have a life*, I thought.

I unconsciously hid my true feelings from myself so well that it was years later before I could acknowledge how guilty I felt because I couldn't be more involved in the lives of my children, even though certain circumstances were out of my control. Instead of owning up to my guilty feelings, I unconsciously took them out on others.

So one reason you may not recognize your guilty feelings is that you hide them from yourself. Another reason you might not be able to identify your own guilt is that you're transforming it by changing it into something more acceptable. Remember, we don't like to see ourselves in a bad light. We don't want to think of ourselves as guilty or guilt-ridden because it implies weakness.

"I feel guilty." When you say it to yourself it doesn't make you feel strong and adequate, does it? It implies that you are shirking some responsibility . . . are not doing what you should be doing . . . are not living up to your potential.

The Stigma of Guilt

Guilt is not something to have; it's something to run from. XM radio is "guilt-free radio"; Chili's restaurant offers the "guilt-free grill." Guilt is so detested in the popular culture that it's no wonder you might decide something else is the source of your misery—you might think that you have low self-esteem, depression, or anxiety. Although these are also difficult emotions, they are much more acceptable these days. They no longer carry the stigma that is still attached to guilt.

Tom's Story

I'll tell you a story about a client of mine that illustrates the emotional pain, confusion, and frustration that occurs when guilt is the source of the problem but the problem is blamed on something else. I first saw Tom on a late November afternoon that was as gray and bleak as his expression. Even though Tom was bright, articulate, and caring, and had been doing every possible thing he could think of to make himself happy, he appeared depressed to everyone, including his physician. His doctor prescribed antidepressant medication and suggested he see a therapist.

As Tom settled himself on the sofa across from me, he picked up one of the soft pillows there and hugged it to his chest. Tom told me he had been depressed for as long as he could remember—not with an incapacitating sadness, but with a nagging melancholy just below the surface. Most of the time he could keep the dark shroud at bay, but it took a lot of energy. When the depression did break through his defenses, he would sink into real despair that lasted from several days to several weeks.

Tom couldn't understand why he was plagued by depression. His life was pretty good. He was a jewelry maker and had designed his own line of jewelry, which he marketed online and at jewelry shows around the country. "If I just had more self-confidence my business could really be something," he said. "I'm just not very good at putting myself out there."

He and his girlfriend had been together for two years. He thought Marcy was probably "the one," although he admitted the relationship was not as satisfying as he thought it could be. "Marcy is a strong woman," he said. "She's very definite in her ideas."

Tom confessed that Marcy rode roughshod over him. "For some reason I can never stand up to her," he said. When there was a disagreement, he'd end up giving in to her just to keep the peace. "I don't know why I do that." He shook his head dismally. "It makes me mad at myself every time. Am I a doormat or what?"

Tom blamed depression for his low self-esteem and inability to stand up for himself to his girlfriend. "If I could just get this depression under control, my self-confidence will come back."

As the weeks went by, I came to know Tom well. He was a passive sort of person who did not have a well-defined sense of himself. It was not difficult to discover that his insecurity had its roots in his family. Tom's father, a successful doctor, had always wanted his only son to become a physician, too. But Tom was never interested in medicine. Art was his passion.

"Art! What a waste! You'll never make a living in art!" was his father's mantra. Although his mother was compassionate and supportive, Tom's desire was to please his father. He told me of the many ways in which he sought his father's approval and acceptance. He learned to play the trumpet in the fifth grade and went on to become a member of the marching band in high school. He played soccer from kindergarten through grade twelve, and excelled. He worked hard in his studies and made the honor society. He did well in college. He even managed to make a living from art after all. But nothing he did won his father's admiration.

During a particularly intense session, Tom admitted feeling guilty all his life for never living up to his father's expectations. He saw himself not only as a failed son, but because his own identity was so tied up with his father's approval, as a failed human being, too. How could a failed human being have self-confidence or the courage to stand up for himself—to his girlfriend or to anyone else?

No wonder he was depressed! The source of Tom's depression was guilt. Once we named the enemy, we could begin to work on this dark and difficult emotion. We discussed his relationship with guilt in every way—familial, spiritual, psychological, and cultural. We explored the guilt-inducing power Tom's father had over him.

Then Tom worked through the five steps of overcoming toxic guilt. When he came to see that guilt was ruining his life, he was able to let go of what his father thought he should be and devote his energy to learning to celebrate himself for the unique person he was. When he could do that, he was more self-confident and found he was able to stand up for himself. As he presented a more solid image to Marcy, he not only felt better about himself, but Marcy had more respect for him as well and their relationship improved.

How Do I Know if It's Guilt?

So let's find out if guilt is the cause of your pain. It should always be a key suspect. Take a look at your anger or sadness and ask yourself if you could be feeling guilty about something. Is guilt lurking in the background?

Maybe it's not. Guilt is certainly not behind every case of anxiety or depression or any number of other psychological ailments—but if you don't even have the notion that guilt could be the culprit, you'll surely miss it if it is. If you do discover that guilt is the villain, you're on your way. If you're still not sure, read on. Naming the enemy may take you a little longer.

Once you've identified the force holding you captive, you must get acquainted with it. Knowing your enemy gives you power over it. The next four chapters will give you a deeper understanding of guilt so that you can know the emotion inside and out.

In the next chapter you'll read some stories about people in difficult situations where both healthy guilt and toxic guilt are operative. You will see how guilt has both helped and hurt those involved. The stories are real, but I have carefully disguised the identities of the people involved, out of respect for their privacy. I have a very high regard for the courageous people with whom I have worked as a therapist and relationship coach.

3

Sorting It Out: Case Studies

Although it would be ideal to organize guilt neatly into "good" and "bad" categories, in real life, guilt is messy. It's not like your tidy silverware drawer with the forks, knives, and spoons all neatly arranged and divided; it's your worst kitchen junk-drawer nightmare. It's a mix of good stuff and bad stuff all jumbled together. We always have a few essentials in our junk drawer that we can't do without. But there's also a collection of unnecessary doodads and gizmos—things we don't need or use but keep around "just in case." Reach in for your whisk—which you often use—and along with it comes that egg-slicer thing, which you never use.

It's that way with guilt. Every situation calls for sorting and untangling. We must learn to tease out the good guilt from the bad, saving what we need and discarding what we don't.

Your situation will have aspects of both good and bad guilt, although you might not have thought about it like that. The following case studies will show you how both good and bad guilt operate at the same time. I'll pick apart the good from the bad to show you how you can do the same for your own situation.

Lynn and Roger: Guilt in a Blended Family

Lynn and Roger listed "marital problems" on the intake form as their reason for seeking counseling. They had been married for six years. It was a second marriage for both. Lynn had a nine-year-old daughter from her previous marriage who lived with them, and Roger had no children.

"I can't live like this anymore," said Roger as their story unfolded. Lynn sat on the sofa across from him staring at the floor. She reached for a tissue to dab at her tear-filled eyes. "I can't either," she whimpered.

Tiffany, Lynn's nine-year-old daughter, was the point of contention. According to Roger, Tiffany ran the household. When Roger made what he considered normal, everyday requests—turn off the TV, go to bed, don't leave the table until everyone is finished eating—she often ignored him or was sassy and disrespectful. In response, Roger would reprimand her and send her to her room. Although Roger wanted a close relationship with his stepdaughter, he was not willing to tolerate her bad behavior.

Lynn seldom backed her husband up. If her daughter misbehaved, Lynn would gently scold her, and then apologize to her later. When Lynn did institute consequences for bad behavior, she consistently reneged before the sentence was served. For example, one evening when the family sat down to dinner, Tiffany covered her plate with her hands and refused to be served, declaring her hatred for meatloaf. Lynn offered a compromise: if she ate everything else (mashed potatoes and broccoli) she didn't have to eat the meatloaf. Tiffany refused. No, she wanted cereal.

The conflict over food was nothing new. Tiffany was seldom pleased with a healthy variety and demanded her favorites: pizza, cereal, hot dogs, and canned spaghetti. Lynn and Roger both agreed that her eating habits were unhealthy and had to change.

Roger took control of the situation and told Tiffany that she could either eat her dinner or be excused from the table; there would be no substitutes. Tiffany flew into a rage and stormed to the family room, where she turned on the TV and cranked the volume up to an earsplitting roar. Roger followed her in, turned off the TV, took possession of the remote, and banished Tiffany to her room.

Later that night Roger caught Lynn sneaking a bowl of cereal into Tiffany's room. The couple had a heated argument after Tiffany was asleep. Roger criticized Lynn for undermining him, and Lynn accused Roger of being unreasonable, cold, and uncompromising. Roger slept in the spare bedroom that night.

At our next session, Roger slumped into the corner of the sofa like an exhausted prizefighter. "I don't want to be the heavy all the time. I'm sick of it—and I'm sick of fighting about it."

By the third session, Lynn was able to acknowledge that Tiffany had way too much power for a child her age. Deep inside, Lynn knew that discipline was an essential part of good parenting.

"I just feel so guilty . . ." Her voice trailed off. "I left her father. He wasn't a bad father—he was good to Tiffany, but I divorced him because I was so unhappy. He remarried and has a son with his new wife. He has devoted himself to that child and seldom even sees Tiffany anymore! I'm sure she feels rejected. I try to make it up to her."

Lynn's guilt was compromising her parenting responsibilities and putting her relationship with her husband at risk. Stuck between placating her daughter and pleasing her husband, Lynn was emotionally drained. Roger felt powerless and discounted, and he wondered where he fit in Lynn's life.

Over the course of our work together, Lynn came to realize that she could not make up for Tiffany's loss of her father—Lynn's job was to be her mother, and to love and discipline her daughter appropriately. We worked on parenting skills, and slowly Lynn was able to let go of her overindulgent behavior toward Tiffany. She also began to validate Roger's role in her daughter's life as an active, responsible stepparent.

These changes did not come without struggle and conflict. Lynn and Roger worked long and hard to adopt a system of discipline. They painstakingly wrote a list of rules for Tiffany and spelled out the consequences for breaking them. When her parents instituted the new plan, Tiffany was not pleased. Her initial response was to ignore the new rules and throw a temper tantrum when the consequences were levied. Although this tactic had worked for her in the past, this time both her parents were outwardly unmoved by the emotional displays.

Tiffany also tried the silent treatment, refusing to speak to her parents if they enforced a rule. They responded by ignoring her quiet defiance and sticking to the consequence. For example, when Tiffany was rude and disrespectful at the table, she was excused to her room, where she was required to spend the next hour. Throwing a fit or refusing to speak to her parents for the rest of the evening didn't change anything. If she did it again the next night, the result was the same. It didn't take long for Tiffany to learn that if she broke a rule she had to face the music.

Lynn was working on the five steps I'll outline for you in this book, and because of Step Three, she was prepared for her daughter's shock and outrage. When the temper tantrums came, Lynn did her best to remain cool and collected. She met the silent treatment with confidence and indifference. Although she felt a certain amount of guilt, she refused to let this emotion dictate her actions. In the end, the family pattern of overindulgence, chaos, and resentment gave way to one of appropriate limit-setting, order, and mutual respect.

Analyzing Lynn's Guilt

Let's separate Lynn's healthy guilt from her unhealthy guilt. Healthy guilt encourages us to consider the needs of others, and Lynn's concern for her daughter's emotional well-being was a good example of that. Lynn chose to divorce Tiffany's father, knowing there would be negative consequences for Tiffany such as not having contact with her father on a daily basis. She was sensitive to her daughter's distress about losing her relationship with her father and tried to be responsive.

But Lynn's healthy guilt became toxic because she felt respon-sible for her ex-husband's bad parenting when she was not. She tried to do the impossible—make Tiffany's pain about her father go away. She thought that if Tiffany had everything she wanted, she would be happy and not notice her father's absence as much. Overindulgence, however, was making Tiffany a difficult child and destroying Lynn's marriage.

Clara: Guilt in Moving on with Life

Clara's husband died a week before their thirtieth wedding anni-versary. I first saw her for therapy two and a half years after his death. A petite woman of fifty-four, Clara looked young for her age, even though her face was a mask of sorrow and there was no light in her very blue eyes. "I can't get over this," she said, tearing up. "I hate every day of my life."

Things didn't change much over the next eight sessions. The depth of her despair and loneliness dominated our conversations. Then something new emerged. She began talking about a man at the fitness center who called regularly to see how she was doing.

"He annoys me," she said one day as she sipped herbal tea in my office.

"Tell me more about him," I said.

"He's divorced—younger than me, and has a grown daughter." She looked at me with mischief dancing in her eyes and sat the cup down gently. "He's attractive enough, I guess . . ." Again, a look from the corner of her eyes—a playful look. She was up to something.

"Oh?" I said innocently.

She went on. "A couple of months ago he invited me to dinner. I was so shocked I could hardly respond!"

"Because he invited you to dinner?"

She frowned at me like the mother of a wayward child. "I'm not ready for that! A date? It's way too soon. It wouldn't be right."

I thought she protested too much. "Too soon?" I feigned surprise.

"Well, I just couldn't!"

"Why not?" I pressed.

"Go out with another man?" She sighed heavily, and a look of hopelessness crept across her face. "In the first place, I would be betraying my husband—the guilt would be too much. In the second place, my kids would never forgive me. My faithfulness to their father's memory is so important to them. I should be ashamed of myself for even talking about another man."

As it turned out, I was right about the spark I saw in my client's eyes; Clara *was* interested in the man at the fitness center. But there was another issue that worked its way into our conversations. My client's religious upbringing made sex outside of marriage a definite taboo. She knew that there were sexual expectations in the adult dating world and was frightened of putting herself in what she considered a morally dangerous situation. If dating meant running the risk of a sexual encounter, she thought it was safer not to date.

"What would happen if you did date, and you did have sex?" I asked.

"I'd go to hell for sure," she said with conviction.

Analyzing Clara's Guilt

Let's stop here to sort out the healthy guilt from the toxic guilt: One reason Clara did not want to start dating was because she knew her children would not approve; their disapproval would make her feel guilty. Part of this was healthy guilt. Healthy guilt encourages us to consider the needs of others—and after all, Clara's children had lost their father and they were suffering. She loved them and wanted to be sensitive to their needs.

But healthy guilt became toxic as time went by. Although the usual grieving period was over, fear of her children's disapproval kept Clara enslaved in a trap. She was not free to do what she wanted to do and had become a victim of toxic guilt.

Healthy guilt helped Clara put restraints on her emotions. Although she was attracted to the man at the fitness center, she felt guilty when she contemplated a relationship with him. This guilt kept her from rushing headlong into a new relationship before she was emotionally ready for one.

However, toxic guilt made Clara blind to the real situation. She felt she would be betraying her deceased husband if she accepted a date with another man. The reality was that Clara's husband was dead, and had been for over two years. Would she really betray her deceased spouse by searching for her own happiness?

Toxic guilt was making her a suffering hero as well. Even though she was sad and lonely, she had a false sense of honor about not being open to the man's attentions when she really wanted to be. The guilt that made her feel ashamed of herself just for being attracted to him was toxic for sure.

Clara was trapped in the throes of anticipatory guilt. Although she hadn't made a move, she didn't think she could bear the guilt if she did. For the next several months we focused on her conflicted feelings. How could she break free from her guilt? How would she deal with her children's disapproval? What would she do if the relationship thrived—how would she handle the sexual part?

As we worked through the five steps of overcoming toxic guilt, Clara and I explored her relationship with her adult children, which was a good one. It was clear that her habit was to support their decisions, and she took care not to intrude in their lives. She did not give advice unless they asked her for it. As we talked about this, Clara came to see that she deserved the same respect from them in return. Her greatest desire was for her children to have a happy and fulfilling life. Wasn't she worthy of happiness and fulfillment too? She decided that she was.

The more difficult conversations were about her religious tenets. She struggled with what she had always been taught but had never questioned: that sex outside of marriage was a sin, period; no questions asked. Now she found that the prohibition seemed unreasonable in the context of her life. After all, she was a widow in her mid-fifties, with a long life ahead of her. I suggested she go deep inside and ponder these questions: What would God say to her about her dilemma? What did God, whom she loved and believed in, want for her?

After much soul-searching, Clara decided that she would at least put her toe in the water. Her first step was to accept a simple dinner date with the man in question. Her children were more accepting of her decision than she had predicted. After so much sadness, they were eager for their mother to find something positive in her life. As it turned out, Clara had a wonderful time on her date and was so enamored of the man that it no longer mattered whether the kids approved or not!

Although I didn't see much of Clara after that, I knew that healthy guilt would cause her to move cautiously before committing to a new relationship.

I'd like to compare and contrast Clara's story with the story of another client in a similar situation. Diana was caught in a guilt trap too, but her path to freedom was very different.

Diana: Guilt Ignored

Diana was a real-estate broker with two children, one in high school and one in college. She had been divorced for eleven years and was having an affair with a married man. He had made it quite clear to Diana that he did not intend to leave his wife. Nonetheless, Diana's world revolved around him. He was loving and attentive, her confidant and mentor. She depended on his support and friendship, and couldn't imagine her life without him.

When I saw her for the first time, I was struck by her outspoken, matter-of-fact attitude. She emanated an aura of independence and self-confidence. One would never guess how uncertain and fragile she was on the inside. She sat quite stiff and straight on the sofa in front of me. "I'm certain that I'm depressed," she said confidently.

"Do you have any idea why you might be feeling depressed?" I asked.

"Not really." She lifted her chin. "I like my work," she pronounced. "Of course, my personal life is a shambles, like everybody else's."

"Maybe you'd better tell me about your personal life."

There was a long silence. Sighing deeply, she told me about her affair. "That's the whole ugly story," she said, scanning my face for signs of disapproval. "What do you say to yourself about being with a man who tells you he will never leave his wife?"

"I say I'm an idiot. I say I deserve more."

Her chin dropped and she slumped a bit.

"Is that the real reason you're here today—you're having an affair with a married man and you know you deserve better?" I countered.

She sank into the sofa like a wrinkled balloon. "Maybe. I don't know. I don't know anything anymore." Her eyes filled with tears.

I handed her a box of tissues and waited.

"I'm just so sad and miserable all the time. I can be fine for a few weeks, and then it's like I trip into this big dark hole. It's awful. Some days I can't even get out of bed." She dabbed at her eyes. "Isn't that depression?"

As more of her story unfolded, I learned that Diana was a religious person. Her parents were pillars of their temple, and she was no less devout. She reared her children as she had been reared; religious observance was at the center of their lives.

Diana carefully folded and unfolded the damp tissue. "I haven't been attending temple activities for months now. I don't even go to services anymore."

"Why not?"

"I just can't. I feel too guilty. The rabbi called and asked what was wrong. She said she was worried about me, and was there anything she could do. I made something up about this being my busy season." She looked up, pain and grief etched in her face. "What I'm doing is wrong, there's no way around it."

"Wrong in what way?" I needed her frame of reference.

She straightened herself. "Morally wrong. Wrong in the sight of God. Wrong in the teachings of my faith."

"You do have a serious problem," I said. "No wonder you're depressed. When you actively and continually violate your own code of ethics, or personal value system, you really beat yourself up. It's as if you are at war with yourself. As I see it, you have two options: either you change your ethical code, or you break it off with your partner."

"Change my ethical code—what do you mean?"

"You find a way to believe that having an affair with a married man is acceptable. You figure out how to justify your relationship so that you're not at odds with your own moral code of conduct."

"And if I can't?"

"Then you have no choice but to end it. If you continue to think it's wrong and feel guilty about it, but do nothing to change things, then you put your emotional health at risk. You're at risk right now."

Diana was so despondent over the situation that I suggested she see her medical doctor to be evaluated for antidepressant medication. She was often in tears, wasn't sleeping well, had lost her appetite, and felt tired every day. I was afraid that if she didn't get some relief from these symptoms, she wouldn't have the emotional energy necessary to work in therapy or make the important decisions she needed to make.

Her doctor did prescribe an antidepressant, which stabilized her emotions, and then Diana and I went to work. I made the same suggestion to Diana that I had made to Clara: I encouraged her to go deep within and search her soul. What would God say to her about her dilemma? What did God want for her?

Diana concluded that there was no way around adultery. It was hurtful, deceitful, and wrong. The God of her understanding would not sanction such a union. After several weeks of working hard in therapy, Diana decided to end the relationship. Initially, she was relieved. She said it was as if a heavy weight had been lifted. She started attending religious services again, arranged to have lunch with friends she had been avoiding, and had a dinner party. She threw herself into her work.

I didn't see Diana after that for a couple of years. Then one day she called for an appointment. The same unhappy woman I once knew sat in my waiting room. She was crying before I got her back to my office. "I can't stand this," she said, tears coursing down her face as she sank heavily into the sofa. "I'm in the same miserable mess I was when I first came here—full circle."

Diana told me that she managed to survive without her partner for about five months before she caved in and contacted him. Things had gone well at first, but then she began to miss him. Finally, she couldn't tolerate the aching loneliness. As much as she wanted to believe that love made their relationship acceptable in the eyes of God, she couldn't. She felt it was wrong in the marrow of her bones, but she couldn't do without him.

After they reunited, Diana fell into the same old patterns. She felt too guilty to be around her friends, and she quit going to temple again for the same reason. The dark depression returned. Nothing in her life seemed to be working.

Diana was a very bright woman. She didn't need to be told what to do again, but like many people, she seemed to need to hear it from someone else.

"You are not listening to your guilt," I said, rather sternly. "It's telling you to change. It's saying that you must do something. You shouldn't ignore it."

"I can't stay away from him," she bemoaned.

"Of course you can. That's a choice."

By the end of the session Diana had vowed to end the relationship again, this time for good. She was faithful to her promise and with the support of continued therapy was able to end the relationship. It was not an easy transition, and she grieved the loss for many weeks. But in the end, Diana found herself feeling free and at peace.

Analyzing Diana's Guilt

Was Diana's guilt healthy or toxic? There is often a fine line between healthy and toxic guilt. Though some may consider Diana's guilt toxic because it caused her stress, pain, and sorrow, I think it was healthy. It was compatible with her personal value system, and it was consistent with her concept of God. It came from the wisdom of her soul, telling her what was right for her.

Her soul had a lot to say. Deep inside, she knew that a relationship with a married man who would not leave his wife was incompatible with her morals and values. She also knew that such a relationship could never affirm or validate her; she would always be a second-class citizen in that position. Her self-respect was at stake.

In addition, she was deceiving another human being (his wife) and living dishonestly. Deceit and dishonesty were not acceptable to her either. Diana's guilt would help her do what she knew she needed to do.

Healthy guilt encouraged Diana to take responsibility for her part in her lover's infidelity. She felt compassion for her lover's wife and thus guilty about her role as the "other woman." If she ended the relationship, her part in the betrayal would be over.

Diana also knew she was putting herself in the position of a second-class partner by playing the role of a mistress. Healthy guilt enabled her to demand more for herself. Diana had lost respect for herself because she was living a life that was against her personal code of ethics. Healthy guilt enabled her to leave the relationship so that she could face herself, her friends, her faith community, and her God with integrity once again. All of these factors contributed to Diana's decision to end a relationship that was destroying her sense of self and her peace of mind.

Vickie: Guilt in Wanting Out

Vickie had been married to Dan for twenty-one years and was miserable. Dan was a nice man. He'd always been good to her, and they'd been close friends. He had a good job, he didn't drink too much, he didn't chase women, and he shared her religious convictions. The problem was, she didn't love him anymore—not the way a wife should love a husband, and she hadn't for years. Vickie sought my counsel to help her decide what to do.

"Do you think I'll ever find a way to love him again?" She fiddled with the silver cross at her throat.

"Tell me again how you feel about him."

She thought a minute. "I don't feel anything about him. I mean, I don't feel anything negative, but I sure don't feel anything positive. Neutral, I guess. The way I'd feel about any nice man I knew. I have to confess though—it's simply awful to live with someone you really don't care about. I feel so guilty about it. There is this one thing . . ."

"Yes?"

"He's weak. That sounds terrible to say, but it's true."

"How so?"

"He doesn't have a—well, *mature*, for lack of a better word—sense of himself. He can't function independently, like a grown-up. Other people have too much influence over him. If he's thinking of doing something, anything, he has to call a couple of friends. I don't care if it's about making a work-related decision, or about deciding where he and I will go on a vacation, he simply can't make a decision by himself. This always bothered me about him, but I thought he'd grow out of it. He never did. In many ways, I feel like I have a child on my hands—I just don't respect him anymore."

"Have you considered marital therapy?"

"Yes, a thousand times, but I never actually suggested it. Maybe I never wanted to put that much energy into the marriage. At this point I know I don't want to do marital therapy—it would be dishonest. I don't want to be married to him anymore. Still, I can't stand the thought of divorcing him. It would kill him." She looked at me directly, a plea for help in her eyes.

"Whatever you do has consequences," I said. "He'll be hurt if you divorce him, and if you don't, you'll spend the rest of your life with a man you don't love."

She gazed out the window, lost in thought. Silently nodding her head in affirmation, Vickie turned to me, and with determination said, "I want out."

"I know," I countered, softly.

"I think I can do this." She straightened herself, backing her words with body language. "But you'll have to teach me the steps for overcoming guilt first."

Analyzing Vickie's Guilt

At this point, I bet you can pick out the healthy guilt from the toxic guilt without me. I'll walk you through the process for the sake of review: Healthy guilt enabled Vickie to stay in the relationship and try to make it work. It mattered to her that leaving would cause her husband pain. It also mattered to her that she had made a sacred vow of marriage—as we've seen, healthy guilt encourages honesty, loyalty, and fidelity.

However, by the time she came to see me, she had been trapped in a dead relationship for years and was not being true to herself. That's not so healthy. Toxic guilt caused her to doubt herself and what she knew deep in her heart—she did not love this man anymore, and she wanted out.

Vickie's situation is not uncommon. Healthy guilt enabled her to honor her vows and stay in the marriage even though she was disappointed and disillusioned, but toxic guilt was causing her to sacrifice her chance of happiness to protect her husband's feelings. This kind of guilt wasn't helping either partner. Vickie's husband deserved a woman who loved him and was glad to share her life with him. As long as Vickie stayed in the marriage, his chance at true love was as remote as hers.

Carol: Guilt for Feeling Responsible

Carol suffered through her husband's two affairs. Each time, when she discovered he was cheating, he repented and she took him back. The first time he was unfaithful she was pregnant with their second child. He blamed his dalliance on her: she had not been interested in sex lately, and he needed it on a regular basis. After all, he was a virile young man. She decided that he did have a point, and she could not imagine how she would manage as a single parent with a toddler and an infant, so she forgave him and took him back.

The second episode of infidelity occurred when Carol went back to school to get her master's degree. When she discovered he was cheating on her, she confronted him. Once again, he blamed his behavior on her. He would not have strayed if she were not so focused on school and the kids. Her lack of attention made him feel discounted and unimportant.

She decided he was probably right that she had been a less-than-adoring wife. He promised to break it off with the other woman, and she took him back a second time.

Three years later, an acquaintance called to tell her about her husband's involvement with yet another woman. By now, Carol was working full-time and the kids were teenagers. Her husband traveled frequently for his work and was meeting the other woman when he was out of town on work-related trips. This time, when Carol told him she knew about the affair, she announced that she was through with the marriage for good.

Her husband fell apart. He begged and pleaded for another chance; he told her how much he needed her. But it was too little, too late for Carol.

The couple divorced. Not wanting to make life difficult for him or the children, Carol decided to keep things as normal as possible. She invited him to holiday events and on vacations. The now-divorced couple talked on the phone frequently, and he dropped by for visits on a regular basis. Carol continued to run his life like she always had—facilitating his relationship with the children, making social arrangements, and running interference for him with his family.

She came in to see me one day and said that her family and friends were complaining that she was overly involved with her ex and was not moving on. Her frustrated sister went so far as to accuse her of being a martyr. Carol was insulted by everyone's meddlesome concern. She needed more time, she said. This was a huge transition after twenty-two years of marriage, and people were expecting too much.

However, a few weeks later when she found herself taking him a cake she had baked late one night, she had an "ah ha!" experience. Her friends and family were right.

She sat in my office, crying. "What's the matter with me? I can't seem to let go. He's got some hold on me!" She reached for a tissue.

"I don't want him. I wouldn't be married to him again for anything, you know that. But he's still in control somehow."

"Carol, you've always run circles around your ex," I said. "You manage all his relationships. Your couple friends were really your friends. You've micromanaged his relationships with the children because he didn't know what to do with them. You were even the mediator between him and his own family! Why do you suppose you have felt so responsible for him?"

She squirmed. "I don't know—I honestly don't."

I was amazed that she could not see what seemed so obvious to me. "Would you be interested in my perception?"

"Of course."

"There's something wrong with this guy. He doesn't take responsibility for his behavior. He can do what he likes and expects to be forgiven. Maybe he has a personality disorder. He's narcissistic or something. I don't know what it is, but something's wrong."

My client was nodding her head sadly. "I know. It's true," she said.

"Is it possible you feel sorry for him—and responsible for him— as you would for a child or someone who was not quite right?"

Her green eyes shone as the truth popped to consciousness. "Oh my god! That's it! I'd feel terribly guilty if I didn't take care of him. I picked him, so he's my responsibility. He may be successful in business, but he doesn't know a thing about relating to people!"

"Well, you don't have to be responsible for him anymore. He betrayed you and you divorced him. It's over."

Carol felt responsible for her husband as one feels responsible for one's child. When she understood that this was the cause of her guilt, she could understand her behavior and see how irrational her thinking had become. Her husband was a grown man. It was time to let him stand on his own two feet.

Analyzing Carol's Guilt

Several aspects of toxic guilt were operative in Carol's story. First and foremost, toxic guilt made Carol blind to what was really going on. The truth was that over the course of her marriage she figured out that she had married a spoiled child. She felt it was her fault; she should have known better than to have married a man who was so emotionally immature. But she did marry him and believed it was her duty to take care of him. When he was unhappy she felt guilty: she must have done something wrong or he would be happy. She wasn't good enough; if she were, he would be happy.

Thus, she was enslaved by him as well. Her life revolved around meeting his needs, and in order to do it, she endlessly gave and gave. Toxic guilt makes us feel responsible when we are not; Carol felt responsible for her husband's happiness and the success of his relationships throughout the marriage. She even continued to take responsibility for his happiness and his relationships after the divorce.

Carol's family and friends pleaded with her to stop taking care of her ex-husband. Instead of heeding their warnings, she continued to play the suffering hero by sacrificing herself on his behalf.

Toxic guilt made her doubt herself as well. A part of her believed that her husband had the affairs in the first place because there was something wrong with her. Happily, once Carol was able to expose the toxic guilt that lurked beneath the surface of her consciousness, she could choose to see things differently. She realized that her husband's infidelity was not her fault and that she was not responsible for him. She also learned that she was not solely responsible for anyone else's happiness.

Now you have a good grip on understanding the nature of guilt and distinguishing healthy guilt from unhealthy guilt. In the next chapter, I'll help you understand the psychological aspects of guilt—why you so quickly and easily feel guilty.

4

The Psychological Underpinnings of Guilt

If you are trapped by guilt, chances are you have a fragile sense of self. In all probability, you are overly dependent on the approval of others and are not very good at taking care of yourself. You may also have poorly defined boundaries and an inflated sense of responsibility. You have to get over it.

The Harmful Consequences of Guilt

I don't mean to sound harsh, but these characteristics of toxic guilt have harmful consequences. They make you subject to burnout in your jobs and your relationships, as well as prone to chronic physical ailments such as arthritis, migraines, digestive disorders (including ulcers and colitis), fibromyalgia, and chronic fatigue syndrome. You are also more vulnerable to conditions resulting from a compromised immune system, like frequent colds, flu, viruses, and allergies.

Toxic guilt caused me to burn out of a variety of jobs. Although I did not realize at the time that toxic guilt was fueling the fire, I did know that I was driven to achieve. At one point in my career, I worked as a counselor for adolescents on a substance abuse ward. I threw everything I had into the job—I felt terribly guilty if I didn't do everything I could and give everything I had to help these kids, many of whom relapsed.

A seasoned psychologist on our staff took me aside one day for some friendly advice: "If you don't quit giving yourself away like this," he said, "you'll burn out in this job and never want to see another addicted teen in your life." Oh, how right he was! In a little more than two years, I was fried to a crisp and never worked with substance-abusing youth again. All because of guilt.

I have had my share of relationship burnouts too. I married a man so needy that I became his emotional life-support system. I constantly bolstered his fragile ego and mended his botched relationships. Trapped by toxic guilt, I assumed responsibility for his happiness and walked on eggshells to avoid upsetting the delicate balance of his moods. Eventually my supply of light and dazzle ran out. Exhausted and resentful, I left the relationship.

I overdid caretaking in other areas of my personal life as well. I had such an immense sense of responsibility that I took on all comers. The result depleted my physical and psychological resources to the point that if it had not been for caller I.D. and other avoidance tactics, I would have self-destructed.

My health even suffered. I have had rheumatoid arthritis, a couple of stomach ulcers, and chronic migraines. I am certain that the stress caused by guilt contributed to these maladies. Fortunately, these debilitating disorders, though still part of my health history, are no longer critical concerns. But dealing with guilt still is.

The psychological underpinnings of guilt are a complicated network of mental and emotional phenomena. Operating concurrently and interdependently, they create an environment in which toxic guilt thrives. Let's go through this network and look at each phenomenon one at a time to see how guilt plays a role.

Self-Concept

Toxic guilt develops at least in part from what you think, feel, and believe about yourself—what mental health professionals call a "self-concept." It's the story you create about who you are. You write the story chapter by chapter as you grow and develop.

The prelude to your story was written by your particular genetic makeup before you were born. You were one of a kind right from the beginning: you may have been a calm baby or you may have been anxious or upset. You could have taken to the breast easily or not. You might have preferred being held only by your parents, or you might have been comfortable in the arms of strangers. As a toddler you might have been hostile and defiant, or passive and compliant. When you were a child you might have been immune to your parents' instructions, or you could have been so sensitive to their directives that your behavior could be controlled by your mother's raised eyebrow.

Although you were unique at birth, the first chapter of your story is the same as everyone else's: you saw yourself as all-important. You thought that you were the center of the universe and that the world revolved around you. However, it did not take long for you to learn that your belief was flawed. Other people's perceptions of you—especially those of your parents—were also very important.

You learned this lesson quite early. If you were squalling and bawling because you had a wet diaper, but your mother thought you were hungry, you got a bottle whether you wanted it or not. You saw your needs one way, but your mother saw them another and responded accordingly.

Your mother's ability to respond appropriately to your needs told you something about yourself. If her response met your needs, you fit comfortably into a world that was friendly, safe, and secure—and you began to feel secure, at least for a while. If your needs were not met, you may have felt like an alien in an unfriendly and unsafe environment.

Thus began the lifelong process of monitoring the way others respond to you. You do it every day, in every interaction. Just as you once scrutinized the way your mother responded to you, you continue to evaluate the reactions of others—facial expression, tone of voice, and body language. You are looking to see your-self reflected and have some of your needs met through the other person's response.

Unfortunately, you do not always get an accurate reflection. As in the example of your mother misinterpreting your crying, the other person can be wrong about what you need. Sometimes the other person is hiding her true feelings from you; she may act one way and feel another. She may be pleasant and cordial when really she finds you a bore.

It is also possible to misinterpret another's response to you. You may think she is angry with you when really she just does not feel well. As imperfect as another person's reflections of you may be, they are logged into the developing story of who you are.

Of course this is all going on while the other person is trying to do the very same thing: get his or her needs met and be validated by you. It is a complicated process, and the possibility of miscom-munication and misunderstanding runs high.

Thus, from birth into adulthood the plot of your story—your self-concept—develops. Some parts of your story record the ways in which you see yourself, while others document how people appear to see you. As your perceptions of yourself and the responses of others merge with your genetic background, you create the story of who you are.

Living with Your Self-Concept

The seeds of your self-concept begin to germinate in the preschool years, although the growth and development of your self-concept is active throughout your life. Sometime during the school years your basic self-concept is formed—and you hang on to it with a death grip.

Just as children love the reassurance of hearing that favorite story over and over again, you feel reassured when your perception of who you are is predictable and does not change. You do not feel safe when your self-concept is challenged.

If someone responds to you in a way that does not fit your self-concept, it is likely you will either misinterpret or twist her response to match the way you see yourself. For example, if you see yourself as unlovable and someone responds to you in a loving manner, you may not let the love in because it does not fit your story.

The character of the Beast in the film and theater rendition of the fairy tale *Beauty and the Beast* saw himself as unlovable and at first could not receive Belle's affection, even though he wanted it. If you, like the Beast, have a self-concept that is rigid and negative, you may rewrite positive or neutral responses from others as negative in order to fit your image of yourself.

On the other hand, the character of Gaston from the same story thought of himself as superior, special, and favored above others. When Belle rejected him he did not see her negative response as valid. After all, who would spurn a catch like him?

If you have a rigid self-concept, you discount the valuable input of others when writing your story. But if your self-concept lacks stability, you will allow others to write too much of it for you. If that is the case, your story of you becomes the "shoulds" and "oughts" of others. You become what you think others want you to be, losing the freedom to define yourself.

Neither a rigid nor a fragile sense of self promotes emotional health. A healthy self-concept is firm but flexible. Others can, and indeed should, influence your story in order for you to grow, but they should not write it for you. People with toxic guilt have a fragile sense of self; they allow others to ghost write too many chapters in the story of their lives.

Approval

Guilt-ridden people want to be liked. They want to be good. They are interested in saying the right thing, doing the right thing, and even feeling the right feelings.

Human beings become invested in being good and getting things right at a very early age. Children behave in ways that they think society or their parents want them to. The desire to get things right continues in life: mothers want to be "good" mothers, fathers want to be "good" fathers, employees want to be good at what they do, and so on.

The culture in which one lives defines what is good and what is right. Depending on the culture, "being good" and "doing the right thing" can encompass a broad range of behavior or may be limited to a very narrow range of behavior indeed. And moral standards of right and wrong or good and bad change and evolve as a culture evolves. In my great-grandparents' day it was socially unacceptable to divorce, no matter what. But divorce today is viewed as acceptable and even good in some circumstances, especially when one divorces an abusive spouse. Owning slaves, once a legal right in the United States, was eventually understood to be morally wrong, and the laws were changed.

The desire to be good and do the right thing serves us well because it provides a societal structure, within which there is stability and order. Taking turns with others at a four-way stop, for example, is the good and right thing to do, and that is currently reflected in our laws. It is not good or right, on the other hand, to talk on your cell phone in a theater after the performance has started—and while this law isn't yet on the books (though there are many who believe it should be), people avoid this behavior simply because it is not a good thing to do, whether it's a law or not.

Feeling good or right about yourself and the things you do helps to solidify a positive self-concept. People with a positive self-concept tend to be healthier and happier than those who have a negative sense of self. People with toxic guilt quickly and easily feel they are not good enough, that they are doing everything wrong. Deep in the psyche of people plagued by guilt lurks a negative self-concept. It's not always a totally negative self-image, to be sure, but if you have enough doubt about getting things right or being good enough, toxic guilt will maintain a prominent place in your self-concept.

Being good and getting approval from others go hand-in-hand. When people are good and get things right, they win the approval of others—and the approval of others feeds a positive sense of self. However, those who suffer from toxic guilt are overly dependent on the good opinion and approval of others. This can be dangerous, since their self-concept is usually either very weak or very strong but negative. If they have even a hint that someone is not pleased with them, they feel guilty, as though they have done something wrong. The guilt-ridden do not want others to see them in a negative light, and they don't want to see themselves that way either.

Those with toxic guilt spend their lives cultivating a self-concept that is consistent with their perception of what a good person is. That perception is rigid and not subject to much leeway. People with toxic guilt want to be as good as good can be.

Random comments like the following cause some people to set unreasonably high standards for themselves:

- "That Marion—what a saint! Just retired, you know, but babysits her granddaughter every day now—eight to five."
- "Son, a man's word is all he has. Everyone knows that only a weak, sorry excuse for a man would break his word."
- "I'd like to introduce the chairman of this year's luncheon series. Linda has worked tirelessly on this project. One by one everyone else fell by the wayside, but Linda was always there, single-handedly pulling all the pieces together. Stand up, Linda!"

- "Marcia knows she has no business dating. She's got those three kids, and they deserve all her attention."

The message is clear. You will win approval by doing some things and lose approval by doing other things. When you win approval, you feel safe and secure because it supports your notion of being good. But falling the least bit short of what you perceive as "good" puts you on a guilt trip faster than anything else—no matter that Marion, Linda, and Marcia in the examples above are letting guilt drive them down the road to emotional and physical burnout! If you live with toxic guilt, you will sacrifice health and well-being in an attempt to support the story that you are good.

The need to think of yourself as good all the time, as well as your rigid high standards of what being good means, can get you into trouble and lead you down the path of toxic guilt. For example, if a man believes (as many do) that honoring his word or promise is an unquestionable prerequisite to being a good man, he is apt to set that standard for himself in stone. What is he to do when he finds himself in a wretched marriage? Chances are he will not consider divorcing his wife because, after all, he made a vow; his guilt will enslave him in a bad relationship.

If a woman believes (as many do) that the care and nurturing of others is the most important requirement for being a good woman, she is apt to sacrifice all else to that end. Should we be surprised that after years of denying her own needs she depletes her emotional resources and becomes ill?

In the Alcoholics Anonymous program, "stinking thinking" is the adage coined to describe the thoughts of substance abusers who perceive themselves as bad and wrong. "Stinking thinking" is a roadblock to recovery and health; members of AA work diligently to change these negative patterns.

If you are trapped in the mire of toxic guilt, you have stinking thinking too. It is stinking thinking when you contemplate doing or saying something that is important to you, but you do not go through with it solely because it would not be well-received by another. It's also stinking thinking when you think—again, on a deep and often unconscious level: if I do (or don't do, or say or don't say) this thing, I won't be a good person, and if I'm not good, that means I must be bad. You feel painfully guilty when you do not live up to your own standards of goodness, even if those standards are unattainable.

As you move through the five steps outlined in subsequent chapters, you will explore how your notion of being good is robbing you of freedom by keeping you guilty. You will also be taking a long, hard look at how much power you have given others to define who you are.

Boundaries

It has been said that good fences make good neighbors, and it's true from an emotional standpoint as well. An emotional fence is a border or boundary that separates your emotions from those of others. It is a marker that designates property—inside the fence, the property is yours; outside the fence, it belongs to someone else.

People of the guilt-ridden variety do not have great emotional fences. Some do not have any. When they do construct fences, they build them too far from the ground, and people tend to sneak under them when they are not watching. Others do not maintain the emotional fences they do have, so that over time their fences fall apart and people just walk right in. Guilty people are also apt to roam around on other people's property when they should not. Assuming responsibility for someone else's territory can be intrusive indeed.

The construction of emotional fences is an important psychological activity. The structure of an emotional fence should be sturdy enough to keep out those who would wander in uninvited, but have enough gates so invited guests can come and go. A fence should not be too high or too solid. One needs to be able to see who is approaching and be accessible to friendly neighbors who may want to visit across the fence.

There are those who build walls instead of fences, and then no one gets in. Alienation and loneliness plague those who build emotional walls.

For the chronically guilty, just the opposite is true. Their fences are too open, and so their lives are replete with people who wander across their territory on their way to somewhere else. They also find themselves in the company of those who have trespassed on their unsecured property to set up rather permanent camps.

Fence-building begins early in life. Children have an abundance of personal property; they think everything belongs to them. Kids are self-focused, the center of their own world. Then the reality of "other" begins to invade their little kingdoms. Little by little, a child's property shrinks as he learns he has to share. Children come to understand that all property must be divided and that everyone needs to know whose territory is whose.

If our primary caregivers and the other important adults in our lives—teachers, coaches, relatives, ministers—do a good job, we learn that marking our territory is important work, and we are validated when we build good fences but not impenetrable walls. On the other hand, if the significant adults in our lives imply that pleasing others is the most important thing, we will not feel comfortable building fences in order to secure our private domain.

Over time, in the noble attempt to please, guilty types allow others to overrun their territory. They voluntarily relinquish their personal space. Conversely, they have trouble honoring the markers of someone else's property. Bent on pleasing others, they let the land on their side of the fence go fallow while they exhaust themselves tilling, planting, and fertilizing their neighbor's ground.

Self-Care

If you have lost the path to health and freedom because of guilt, you are neglecting to care for and protect yourself. Everyone needs self-care skills, but people in a fog of toxic guilt cannot discern the difference between self-care and "self-ish." In an attempt to avoid the evil of selfishness at all costs, the guilty err on the side of selflessness, placing the needs of others above their own needs. In order to be healthy—emotionally and physically—all of us need to tend our own fires. We need to refuel and nurture ourselves.

Refueling and nurturing requires time, solitude, and the freedom to take care of ourselves as we see fit. Healthy individuals balance their own needs with the needs of others; the guilt-ridden do not. If you are emotionally depleted, physically drained, and angry and resentful, you are not much use to anyone.

Although both men and women who are laden with guilt have difficulty taking care of themselves, it is particularly problematic for women. Women are conditioned to believe that their value is defined, at least to some degree, by how well and how much they give. Many women are hypersensitive to the tiniest possibility that their behavior might be construed (by themselves or by others) as being self-indulgent. Remember, people want to get it right. If a woman believes that good women are selfless, she will go all-out to fit that mold.

What we all need, and women most of all, is a restored sense of balance. On one end of the giving continuum is narcissism—self-absorption, lack of empathy, arrogance, grandiosity, and a sense of entitlement. Narcissism is a mental disorder; some would call it a sin. The other end of the continuum—overidentification with the needs of others, lack of self-respect, inability to set personal limits, an inflated need to please, and poor self-care skills—is equally soul-shocking. Somewhere in the middle is balance: the ability to nurture, respect, and care for the self while remaining profoundly open and receptive to the needs of others.

The emotional cost of exaggerated selflessness—hostility, anxiety, and guilt—is high. Yet how quickly many people translate healthy attitudes of self-care into specters of selfishness and indulgence!

The airlines have this figured out. As the plane taxies down the runway, the flight attendant instructs passengers on what to do should oxygen be needed. Passengers are told that if they are traveling with anyone who needs assistance, they should take care of themselves first before securing the oxygen mask for the other. Obviously, if the strong person is oxygen-deprived, he or she will not be much good to the weaker one.

Here is another metaphor that illustrates the importance of self-care. Imagine an old wishing well, complete with bucket and rope. When you draw water from the well, the bucket goes down and repeatedly brings up water. What happens over time if you keep drawing the water? The well goes dry, right? Yes, unless there is an underground spring or body of water that is a constant source of replenishment.

People who give and give, without securing resources for themselves from which to draw, go dry as well. The result is anger, bitterness, resentment, or depression and other physical illnesses.

Responsibility

Guilty people assume responsibility for others. At the drop of a hat, they feel obligated and duty-bound. They feel that way partly because they want to please, partly because they want to be able to think of themselves as good, partly because they have poor boundaries, and partly because they aren't meeting their own needs well.

Being overly responsible feeds toxic guilt, and toxic guilt feeds being overly responsible. If you are an overly responsible person with toxic guilt, you will not think, feel, or behave in the same way as someone who is free of this burden.

Imagine what your response would be to a friend who needs help moving on a weekend to which you have been looking forward for rest and relaxation. If you are free from toxic guilt, you can be honest with yourself and your friend. You can simply not volunteer to help, or you can explain that in order to take care of yourself, you have to bow out this time. Then you would be free to relax and enjoy your weekend.

If you are trapped by toxic guilt, you'll feel it is your responsibility to help your friend. Maybe you will picture yourself working away and think about how grateful your friend will be. You will probably think it's your duty to help, no matter what—after all, what are friends for? You may be afraid of what your friend will think of you if you don't help. You're sure that even if you manage to resist the urge to volunteer, you still won't be able to enjoy your weekend; every time you think of what you really should be doing, a surge of guilt will course through you like an electric current. Since you know you won't be able to rest and relax, you pick up the phone and offer to help, saying you had nothing else planned.

In this chapter you learned how your self-concept, need for approval, ability to establish good boundaries, self-care skills, and sense of responsibility play vital roles in the formation of toxic guilt. In the next chapter we will turn our attention to what's going on between you and the people who seem to be experts at making you feel guilty.

5

The Dynamics of Guilt

It has been said that those who can make us feel guilty own us. That's because guilt is energy that has the potential to control behavior. Who are the people that use guilt to control others, and who are the people that are easily controlled by them? This chapter explores the interplay between victims and rescuers, two personality types that together unleash toxic guilt.

Victims and Rescuers

Victims are emotionally wounded people who use guilt to manipulate others, and rescuers are people who are intent on helping them. Since the psychological dynamic between the two is an essential component of toxic guilt, it's worth taking a look at both of these personality types here.

Victimhood is the bedrock of some people's personalities and self-concepts. You're bound to know someone who is an accomplished victim—and an expert at making you feel guilty as a result. Real victims are people who both need and deserve help, but there are also those who imitate real victims. I call them pseudo-victims. If you are a rescuer, pseudo-victims have power over you because they know how to trade on your sensitivity to their neediness. They will use this power to manipulate and control you.

It can be quite difficult to discern a real victim from a pseudo-victim, but it is essential to learn how to tell the difference. When you learn to distinguish a real victim from a pseudo-victim, you will be free to respond to those who really need your help and free to resist those who don't.

Real victims are either born—children with physical and/or mental disabilities—or made—children abused or neglected by their families and others; people deprived of cultural opportunities because of poverty, race, gender, or sexual identity; hardworking individuals faced with financial problems due to natural disaster, war, or national economic conditions; widows and orphans; the unjustly accused; and those who are struck by catastrophic illness or injury. Pseudo-victims are those who could overcome the adversities of their lives and move forward but choose not to. Rather than take responsibility for improving their lot in life, they look to others to make life easier for them.

When you were a child, you probably had some experience of being a victim. If you were bullied at school, pushed into the deep end of the pool before you could swim, or spanked for something your brother did, you were a victim. Some of these childhood injustices stick out in our mind because they were unusually painful, but most are lost in the oblivion of everyday life lessons.

As adults, frightening events and disappointments continue to make us feel victimized, but we know how to respond. When someone is abrupt or rude to us it may hurt our feelings a bit, but we tell ourselves to ignore it, and we go on. We're able to handle the ordinary ups and downs of life.

It is easy to see that people who are not protected as children are victims of neglect. It is not as obvious that people who are overindulged or over-soothed as children are victims as well. Although it is almost impossible to overindulge or over-soothe a baby (who should get as much attention as he or she needs), it is very possible to overindulge or over-soothe a child.

Parents or caregivers who overindulge or over-soothe do not provide the necessary experiences that promote emotional growth. Children need the emotional trials and tribulations that teach independence and self-sufficiency; when they do not get them, they are, in a way, neglected. Therefore, in terms of development, too much caregiving equals neglect and can just as easily lead to victimhood.

When children are not disciplined, comforted, soothed, and attended to by their parents according to what they need, they emerge from childhood feeling incomplete. It is as if they carry an empty space inside that longs to be filled. A neediness permeates their personality, and they may spend their lives in victimhood, searching for someone to save them from their emptiness.

Certainly, people who do not get adequate or appropriate emotional care as children are real victims. However, no one has to stay stuck in the disappointments of childhood. I'll discuss that in a minute.

Children who receive excessive attention and affection when they are victimized ("Oh, you poor dear! Let me take care of that for you!") also learn to be victims. A child who is rewarded for being a victim will have difficulty moving out of the role of victim as an adult.

On the other hand, children praised and rewarded predominantly for being responsible ("She's so grown-up for her age! You're such a little man!") are set up to become rescuers. If you got praise and attention as a child for having the qualities of a rescuer, then you are apt to continue to be a rescuer as an adult.

A situation in which a child must function in an adult role is also fertile ground for growing rescuers. For example, my client Nancy was placed in such a situation at age thirteen, when her father left her mother for another woman and her mother then attempted suicide. Nancy became a "little soldier," the defender and protector of her emotionally fragile mother. Later in life,

Nancy's sense of responsibility for her mother became a guilt trap. How could she move to another state with her husband when her mother needed her?

A child with an alcoholic or drug-addicted parent may assume adult responsibilities that the parent is unable to perform. The same can be true for a child whose parent is ill. The disappearance of a parent through death or divorce can place the child in the role of an adult "rescuer" as well.

Michael's mother put him at the head of the table when she and his father divorced. "Now you're the man of the house," she said. Michael was only fourteen at the time and had two younger sisters. When he was older, dating was a nightmare for him. The responsibility he felt for his mother and sisters was transferred to every girl he dated—how could he be the one to inflict pain? He almost gave up dating altogether because the guilt he felt by not calling a girl back for another date, let alone breaking off a relationship, was too much to bear.

Everyone is a victim at times, and everyone is a rescuer at times. Both roles are a normal part of the human condition. Healthy people reach out to others for help when they need to and take care of others when it is appropriate. But many people develop personalities that are predominantly one role or the other. Hence, there are those who seem to be victims most of the time (the pseudo-victims) and those who seem to always be rescuing others. Each role has its payoffs and liabilities, and each can play an important role in toxic guilt.

The perks of being a pseudo-victim are high. Not much is expected from people who are perpetual victims. They are excused from responsibility, continually let off the hook. Others step in and take care of them, making their decisions and solving their problems.

The price can be equally high. Chronic pseudo-victims aren't taken seriously; they are relegated to the status of children. Exaggerated dependence on others robs people stuck in victimhood of independence and self-sufficiency. Many people eventually leave persistent pseudo-victims because of their oppressive dependence and neediness. Pseudo-victims who want to change because they are insecure, lonely, and unhappy face an uphill battle. They must reshape parts of their personality with grit and intention. This process may require the help of a therapist, but it is well worth it. Unfortunate childhood events need not determine the course of a life.

If you spend most of your life on a guilt trip, it is likely that the needs and expectations of others will map the course of your journey. How do you feel if you don't immediately respond to a call for emotional help from someone? Feeling responsible for making things better, you rush to the rescue whether you want to or not.

Most people reading this book are rescuers—and rescuing has its rewards. When we rescue, we get to be the good ones; we feel influential and sometimes, well, sort of holy. Relieving the pain of others improves life on the planet and strokes our egos at the same time. There's nothing wrong with that, but perpetual rescuers eventually run amok. We end up harming ourselves by exhausting our physical and emotional resources. We burn out, get depressed, and become resentful.

Most rescuers are not aware of another hidden liability. Is it possible that you rescue others in an attempt to meet your own needs? Think about it. Do you give others what you want for yourself? The very things a victim seeks—attention and affection—can also be the goals of those of us intent on rescuing others. The problem is that it doesn't work. Victims usually do not have attention and affection to give back.

The movie *You Can Count on Me* is a great example of the rescuer syndrome. It is the story of Sammy, a working single mother trying to create a good life for herself and her young son. However, she is tangled up with three men. Sammy takes in her ne'er-do-well brother, is in a relationship with a man she does not love, and is having an affair with her married boss. After a series of misadventures, she seeks the counsel of her pastor and tells him the whole sordid story. The pastor says, "Why do you think you're in this situation?" Sammy replies, "Which one?" The pastor says, "All of them." She thinks a minute and responds, "Because I feel sorry for them." In the rest of the movie, we see Sammy freeing herself from all three men.

Pity and guilt fuel the behavior of chronic rescuers. Feeling responsible for the happiness of others, we experience guilt when we do not respond to every need. The key to recovery from knee-jerk rescuing is discernment—the ability to know and be able to choose when to rescue and when not to rescue.

Learning not to respond will not be an easy lesson. Rushing to rescue comes naturally, so not rescuing will go against the habits of a lifetime. Holding back will be a fight—not just with the people who are used to being rescued by you, but also with yourself. It means learning to let go of trying to control other people and learning to let go of the outcome of events you really don't have control of anyway. Even as letting go sets you free, it will evoke a struggle.

You will be faced with a daunting task—the reshaping of your personality. Rescuers, like pseudo-victims who want to change, must reshape parts of their personality with grit and intention. I will do my part to help you do just that in Chapter 18.

Plugs and Receptacles

Sometimes I think of people as either plugs or receptacles. "Plugs," or pseudo-victims, are those who search for energy and power from another. "Receptacles," or rescuers, are people who seem to have an innate source of energy and power to offer. They are open to the needs of others and give of themselves. The trouble is, human beings don't have unlimited energy.

Human energy is a precious and limited resource, and it matters how we use it. It matters who gets our energy, and how often, and how much. There are safety covers for receptacles; rescuers need the same protection. Unfortunately, most of us caretaker types feel terribly guilty if we deny anyone access to our energy.

People Who Make You Lie

I'd like to share a quick story that illustrates the power of pseudo-victims over rescuers. I bet it will sound familiar:

Two women were at a dinner party, talking about a mutual acquaintance. Evidently the woman in question was extremely sensitive and her feelings were constantly being hurt. She was also an expert at letting you know when you were the offender.

"She's one of those people who make you lie," said one woman to the other.

"Exactly!" her friend replied. "She asked what I was doing tonight, but I couldn't tell her I was going to this party. It's not even my party—I'm just a guest—but I knew she would feel discounted and rejected if she knew she wasn't included. If I was the one who told her about it and she knew I was going, I'd feel responsible. I don't need the guilt, so I lied. It's just easier."

Those of us on perpetual guilt trips should never underestimate how sensitive we are to the pleas of a pseudo-victim—no matter how subtle. A heightened sense of responsibility causes guilt to swell if we don't respond. Guilt grips us when we don't answer the phone, when we go to the gym after work instead of straight home, when we cancel a lunch date or leave our teen's underwear where he dropped it on the floor. Guilt makes us lie, too.

The Dance

Rescuers and pseudo-victims are locked in a perpetual dance. When the music starts, the partners step to the floor and grasp each other in the familiar hold. They move together flawlessly, their steps a perfect series of point and counterpoint. Nothing in the dance will change until one of the partners refuses to participate.

In his book *Freidman's Fables*, Rabbi Edwin Freidman tells a story that illustrates the power of the dance between rescuer and pseudo-victim. I'll tell the tale as I understand it:

With excitement and a sense of adventure, a man takes off on the journey of a lifetime. He is determined to discover the meaning of his life and to answer the questions that have long stirred in his thoughts: Who am I? Why am I here? What is my purpose?

His quest takes him over hill and vale and, finally, to a bridge that traverses a great gorge. As he begins his trek across the bridge, he looks up to discover that someone has stepped onto the bridge from the other side. In a few minutes, the two meet in the middle. The other traveler has a rope tied and coiled around his waist. He holds the end of the rope in his hand.

"I need you to take the end of the rope," says the stranger, extending his hand. "Please hold it tightly." The man does as instructed and grasps the rope.

With that, the stranger jumps from the bridge, the rope unwinding as he tumbles about thirty feet. The man grips the rope with all his might and steadies himself against the stranger's weight. Then he makes his way to the side of the bridge and peers over. The stranger is hanging from the bridge, swaying on the end of the rope.

"What's the matter with you—are you crazy?" the man on the bridge screams to the dangling stranger below.

"If you let go of the rope I'll fall to my death," the stranger shouts back. "I am your responsibility now—my life is in your hands!"

Shocked and amazed, the man turns his attention to securing the rope. By now his hands are tired, so he ties the rope around his waist and eases himself into a sitting position to study his predicament. He contemplates going for help, but there is nothing on the bridge to tie the rope to.

Time passes. The man is getting tired and hungry. Once again he calls out to the stranger hanging from the other end of the rope. "I can't do this!" he cries. "I'm on the journey of a lifetime, and I must keep going. I'm tired and hungry, and the rope is burning my skin. You have to do something!"

The stranger looks up. "You must hold the rope! If you don't I will surely die."

Time passes. The man holding the rope removes it from his waist. The rope has rubbed his skin raw, leaving it sore and bleeding. He wraps the rope around his hands and then braces himself against the side of the bridge and hangs on.

Time passes. Now the man is stiff and sore and hungrier than he's ever been. Suddenly, it occurs to him that he is doing all the work; the stranger is not doing anything to help himself. "You're going to have to do something!" he yells at the stranger. "I'm doing all the work here and I'm exhausted! Roll yourself up to the bridge by pulling on the rope and twisting it around your waist."

The whine of a spoiled child comes from below. "I can't do that! I'm not strong. My life is in your hands, and if you drop me I will surely fall to my death!"

The exhausted man has another idea. "I'll give you until sundown to pull yourself up," he shouts. "If you don't, I'm going to drop the rope."

"You surely wouldn't do such a thing!" wails the stranger. "I am your responsibility."

"Oh yes I will," replies the man, his voice icy with resolve. "I mean every word I say!"

Time passes and sundown comes. The man looks over the bridge to see the stranger still dangling helplessly from the rope. He sighs deeply, frees his hands, and continues his journey.

The man in the story did what he could to save the stranger, but when the stranger stubbornly hung on to his victim status by refusing to take action on his own behalf, the man let him go.

Was the man on the bridge a bad person? Was he wrong to let the man fall? Are you now or have you ever been in a similar situation? The dance ends when the pseudo-victim or the rescuer does something new. I'll talk more about letting go in Chapter 18.

To conclude this chapter, I'd like to share another story. The situation of my friend Molly illustrates how self-concept, the need for approval, poor boundaries, inadequate self-care, an inflated sense of responsibility, and the psychological dynamic between pseudo-victim and rescuer all contribute to toxic guilt.

Molly's Story

Molly asked if I would have lunch with her; she needed some advice. I met her at a stylish little tearoom. After ordering, she launched into a tale about a woman in her life—someone she found herself dealing with in a variety of situations—who was making her crazy.

Molly complained that she felt awful about herself because she could never stand up to this person. "I hate how I am with this woman!" She stirred her iced tea, a frown clouding her usually sunny expression. "I let her run all over me." It was not like Molly to say bad things about others.

"She intimidates you?"

"Totally. And I'm a grown-up—or thought I was. She's pushy, bossy, and arrogant. I'll sit there in a meeting with her and watch her take over every time. At least I'm not the only one who can't get a word in! But it's gotten to me—I feel like a spineless worm. What's wrong with me?"

"Nothing's wrong with you," I answered. I knew Molly; there wasn't anything wrong with my friend. "You just have some things to sort through. Take a guess at why you don't stand up to this person."

"I think I don't want the fallout. No, I don't have the energy to deal with the fallout."

Molly was a peacemaker. She was a gentle soul and loved by everyone who knew her. It was hard to imagine her in a head-to-head confrontation. "Have you tried to stand up to her at all? Ever?"

"Well, I have thought about it. I actually practiced what I would say to her. I even enlisted a couple of friends who agreed to be with me when I talked to her—you know, reinforcements. But when the time came, I couldn't get the words out."

"Maybe you feel guilty." (I was working on this book, so guilt was at the forefront of my mind.)

"Guilty?" She looked at me as if I were an alien. "No, it doesn't have anything to do with guilt."

OK, I had missed that one, so I decided to try another approach. "Tell me what this woman is like. Does she have any redeeming qualities? Is she funny? Smart?"

She leaned even closer. "That's just it! She's smart and creative. Most of the time, she really does have great ideas. I can't help but admire her. I even like her."

That comment gave me an idea, and I told her about an old friend of mine. Jamie and I had known each other since childhood. I loved her. She was bigger, stronger, funnier, and braver than I was. She was not afraid of anything or anyone.

Jamie had her own horse and took care of him all by herself. She taught me how to smoke cigarettes in the hayloft of her barn. She made prank phone calls to the teachers we did not like. We had great times together.

But Jamie also terrorized me. She would pin me down and tickle me unmercifully. She said mean things to me. Sometimes she humiliated me in front of other kids, and I took it because I admired her.

As we became adults, nothing much changed. Like the woman Molly was struggling with, it was Jamie's way or no way. I accommodated her as best I could, but finally I stood my ground. The issue was my relationship with her mother. Jamie and her mother had always had a disastrous, conflict-ridden relationship. After high school Jamie left home to attend college in another state and never came back. Eventually, she terminated contact with her mother forever. On one hand, I understood Jamie's decision to cut her mother out of her life—it was right for her. On the other hand, I cared for her mother very much and did not want to end *my* relationship with her, and so I didn't.

After many years, a confrontation occurred. Jamie called me in a rage one night and made it clear that she did not want me to stay in contact with her mother. At that point, I drew a line in the sand. I could not and would not allow her to dictate my relationships and told her so. I never heard from her again. Years later I saw her at her mother's funeral, but we did not speak. I grieved the loss of my friendship with Jamie, but I did what I had to do for myself.

Molly had been listening to every word. "How did you know when to draw that line in the sand?"

"When accommodating her meant giving up too much of me," I said. I explained that it took a long time to reach that point for two reasons. First, Jamie was extremely sensitive; she could not tolerate criticism on any level. She would be deeply hurt if I were to say anything. She would leave the relationship and blame its failure on me, which would make me feel guilty.

Second, I knew that deep in her core, Jamie was insecure and unstable. If I confronted her, it would cut her to the quick. I did not want to be responsible for that because I'd feel even guiltier.

A look of astonishment crossed Molly's face. "That's it! That's exactly it! This woman is just like that. She can't tolerate anyone who doesn't agree with her—it would blow our relationship out of the water if I confronted her. I'm sure she'd never speak to me again.

"She's sensitive, fragile even. I would hurt her. I'd feel guilty. So it's not because I'm so weak of character or screwed up. It's because I'd feel so guilty if I stood my ground. It would be the end of our relationship. I'd hurt her, and then I'd feel like a bad person. Yes—you're right. It is guilt."

"So, what are you going to do?"

She was silent as she folded and refolded her napkin. "I need to decide if I've had enough. If I have, I'll do what I have to do. I'm not going to let her dictate what I do anymore. Then again, I might not do anything. A relationship with her may be worth just going along like I always have. At least I have some choices now."

An Analysis of Molly's Guilt

Molly's sense of self was threatened on two levels. On one level, her relationship with the woman was at stake. If she was confrontational the woman certainly wouldn't like it. She would be most displeased with Molly and might even pull out of the relationship.

For people who value relationships highly, losing even one relationship can be traumatic. Molly saw herself as a "relationship person"—remember, she got along with everyone. If she confronted the woman and the woman left the relationship, Molly would feel as if she had failed or done something wrong. Guilt arises from a sense of doing something wrong.

On the other hand, allowing the woman to have her way all the time threatened Molly's sense of self. Was she really a spineless worm? Molly's relationship with herself was at stake; she felt guilty for being a coward.

Although Molly felt she was the victim in this situation, in reality she was the rescuer and the other woman was the pseudo-victim. She was protecting the difficult woman's fragile self-esteem by allowing her to have her way.

Now that Molly knew that guilt was keeping her stuck, she had options. If she didn't confront the woman, she would not see herself as a weak character now. She would know she was making an informed choice about how to respond, and that put her in charge. Conversely, she could decide that she had been protecting the woman for far too long and that the time had come to make a stand.

Before Molly could name guilt as the source of her problem, she floundered around in her predicament, at the mercy of her emotions. Naming the enemy put her in charge of the situation.

Molly was also able to shed light on the situation by figuring out how her sense of self was being threatened. She needed to find a way to feel good about herself. As it turned out, she had several options, none of which would interfere with her self-concept as a good person.

If Molly were to behave in a way that was not consistent with her notions of what a good person does, she would feel uncomfortably guilty at best and downright miserable at worst. And since having good relationships with others is important to Molly, a lot was at stake for her. Losing even one relationship is frightening for a person who looks for others' approval to validate a positive sense of self.

Now that you understand the roles of victim, pseudo-victim, and rescuer, you are in a position to make better choices about how you will respond when others make you feel guilty. In the next chapter, you will learn that the roots of guilt go beyond genetics, psychological development, and the combination of certain personality types. Culture also influences the formation of toxic guilt.

6

The Cultural
Underpinnings of Guilt

As we've seen, the roots of toxic guilt lie deep in the soil of the psyche and are nourished by genetics and family upbringing. But cultural influences also contribute to an overabundance of guilt. Culture gives meaning to the life of a society and affects the way an individual experiences the world.

For example, I grew up never seeing a banana unpeeled except in one way: the banana is grasped with the stem end up. Then one day my very bright step-grandson, Colin, banana in hand, introduced me to another option. He held the banana with the stem end down and pinched what I would call the bottom of the banana open. It peeled easily. Suddenly, all I had known about peeling a banana was in question. I tried Colin's method and peeled the banana from the "wrong" end. Sure enough, it was easier to break open. I determined to change my ways, but, try as I might, I discovered it was almost impossible for me to develop the habit of doing it Colin's way because it felt so strange and unnatural.

For some, chronic guilt may be as natural as peeling a banana from the stem end. If you suffer from toxic guilt, it may not be because you come from a fatally flawed family or have an unhealthy psyche. The family you grew up in may be only semi-flawed, like most families, and your psychological health may be as good as most. Cultural influences could very well be magnifying what would otherwise be a usual dose of guilt.

How Culture Influences Guilt in Women

Overall, women struggle with guilt more than men. That is because women's behavior is so narrowly defined in our culture. Women must behave very carefully in order to meet the requirements of being "good." Good women are supposed to be nurturing, giving, sympathetic, understanding, and accommodating.

Men are allowed a much wider range of behavior. For example, a man who stands up for himself and does not back down is usually admired and considered "strong," while a woman who does the same is often criticized and considered a "bitch." Assertive behavior in women may be admired, but it is also suspect. It doesn't take much for assertive behavior to be considered aggressive—and aggressive behavior in women is a death sentence for acceptability.

Therefore, women feel they must constantly monitor themselves and take care not to step too far out of line. Many women feel immediately guilty if they have an inkling they have gone too far. The guilt rushes in so fast that they don't evaluate it or consider that what they are feeling might be unreasonable. They don't even think about *why* they feel guilty, they just do. Let's call it knee-jerk guilt.

There are many ways in which our culture defines what a good woman is. For example, good women have children. Women who chose not to have children, for their own reasons, often feel guilty about their decision.

Good women are pleasant, positive, and cheerful. When a woman is not pleasant, positive, and cheerful, the common attitude in the general culture is that the woman is a bitch, an ice queen, or nuts—although the same behavior in men is usually excused. Many women feel guilty every time they simply have a bad day.

The "Supermom" stereotype supports the myth that women should do it all. Over half of the women in the United States are in the workplace—most because of financial necessity—but those who are mothers are still expected to do the majority of the parenting. Although fathers are more involved in rearing children than ever before, mothers still carry the heaviest load and *are expected to*, according to cultural norms. As a result, most working mothers struggle with guilt for not being all they think they should be for their kids.

Additionally, when a woman works outside the home, her husband often still expects her to take care of all of the domestic chores because it is "women's work." She may believe the same thing, feeling she *should* be managing the household by herself and becoming guilty if her performance is not up to par.

When children misbehave or don't do well in school or socially, it is the mother that is usually blamed. This is such an ingrained cultural norm that women often blame other women when they learn about a child's troubles, without even thinking about it. It is no wonder that women feel so responsible for how their children turn out and feel terribly guilty if anything goes wrong.

If a woman finds herself in one of the eight guilt-inducing situations I describe in Part II, cultural messages and myths influence the guilt she feels. If she contemplates leaving a relationship, doing something her parents would not approve of, standing up to controlling family members, or coming out, she faces the guilt of behaving in a way that is out of step with the cultural definition of what a good woman should do. And although a cultural war wages about how we should regard a woman with an unwanted pregnancy, the hostility and hatred of those against abortion portray women who make that choice as unacceptable in every sense of the word. And since the cultural message is that women are responsible for how their children turn out, it is no wonder they feel guilty if their children aren't successful in every way.

How Culture Influences Guilt in Men

Men also struggle with guilt, and toxic guilt gets a foothold on many. The cultural messages are that men should be strong (think hunters and athletes), winners (athletes, warriors, politicians), protective (kings and rulers), and loyal (Boy Scouts and soldiers).

Adult men have a tough time feeling manly these days. They do not have many milestones of maleness. Boys still have organized sports, where muscle, brawn, and agility are measured as they meet the "enemy" in front of admiring onlookers. Boys can pursue concrete goals. They can achieve good grades, get a job, and compete for the affection of a girl. They have numerous other milestones: learning to drive, being welcomed as adults into their faith, graduating from school, going to college, joining the military.

Symbols of success are few and far between for grown men. Since women have joined the workforce, their dependence upon their husbands has greatly decreased. Being the sole provider for the family is no longer the universal standard for masculine success. About all that men have to measure their status is their financial success or a career that provides fame, respect, or power—and there aren't many of those. Most men are regular guys with regular jobs.

Other than financial success or a spectacular career, there seem to be only three cultural standards left that define the male code of honor: a man's word, his sense of responsibility, and his ability to be successful in a relationship. If he falls short in any of these areas, guilt rolls in.

Toxic guilt in men is expressed in a particular dynamic that I often see when working with couples. The woman complains that her partner withdraws whenever there is conflict. "He just clams up and refuses to talk!" she'll say. "I'm so frustrated and angry I could scream!"

Usually, the woman is highly verbal (as a whole, women are more verbal than men). She talks and complains, piling the verbiage on a platter that she presents to her partner. Then she stops and watches him intently, waiting for his response.

He doesn't even know where to begin. He's not feeling very strong, and he knows he's not going to come out ahead on this, so he throws down the trump card by withdrawing. She has no place to go with the discussion, so he wins.

One wouldn't guess that toxic guilt is behind this dynamic, but it is. People feel guilty for falling short of their own expectations. The culture tells a man that he should be a winner, and if he doesn't live up to that standard—even in his own mind—he feels guilty. In this case, withdrawing seems like the best solution, but it puts an intimate relationship in harm's way. Women leave relationships in droves because their men are emotionally distant and refuse to engage.

The impact of the cultural definition of maleness can be seen in the response of men who find themselves in an unhappy marriage. Many men take marriage exceedingly seriously—they took a vow and gave their word. When a man is miserable in his marriage but believes honoring his commitments and remaining loyal is a crucial mark of his manhood, it is almost impossible for him to consider divorce.

Many men feel intense guilt when they contemplate divorce, because they believe it will mean they are failures. The fear of seeing oneself as a failure or of being seen as a failure by others keeps many a good man in a miserable marriage. This is borne out statistically. Significantly more women than men file for divorce.

I believe the reason men are loath to file is that in legal terms the one who files becomes the "petitioner," and the one who answers becomes the "respondent." When a man files and becomes the "petitioner," the prevailing mentality (among men) is that he has failed; he is responsible for not being able to make it work. After all, he's the head of the household.

In the mind of many men, when the wife files for divorce, it means *she* left *him*. Therefore, he is not breaking his word or abandoning his family, and his manliness remains intact. This is a mythical and symbolic perspective. In most states, it doesn't matter *who* files for divorce; there's no legal consequence. But this is not a legal issue, it's a psychological issue.

There is an ugly side to this coin. There are men who want out of their marriage but refuse to file first because of their own big egos. These guys (earning the status of "jerk") will make their wives so miserable that the wives will file just to stay sane, or safe.

When a man confronts one of the eight guilt-inducing situations, cultural expectations have an important influence on his struggle. If he wants out of a relationship, he risks seeing himself as weak because he is not protecting those close to him. He might also think of himself as disloyal and a failure.

This manifests itself in a number of ways. If he wants out from under the thumb of a parent, he may feel like a disloyal or irresponsible son. A man expects to be the example his children strive to live up to, and when they don't, he feels inadequate or like a failure as "head of the household." It is culturally unacceptable for a man to have feminine characteristics, and so coming out as a gay man evokes weighty guilt. Leaving an oppressive faith tradition evokes the guilt of not being strong enough to stay and make things different. It also calls to question a man's sense of being right: *what if they're right and I'm wrong?*

Since guilt itself is considered unmanly, it often masquerades as anger in men. Thus it is anger or righteous indignation that characterizes the behavior of many men who leave relationships, stand up to a parent, come out, corral an unruly child, or break free from an oppressive religious community.

How Culture Influences Guilt over Parents

Our culture has clear messages about how we should feel and behave toward our parents. We disparage children who do not meet the standard for good sons and daughters:

- Our family would never put a parent in a nursing home.
- You should hear the way he talks to his mother—unforgivable!
- We can't not go—Mom and Dad expect all of us to be there.

Mother's Day and Father's Day are national holidays that have spawned commercial enterprises and religious activity. The greeting card and floral industries have capitalized on holidays that honor parents, and retailers encourage gift-giving related to both mothers and fathers. On those special Sundays, sermons and songs commemorating (and idealizing) parents ring out. In every way, we are reminded how much we value and owe our parents.

"Owe" is the operative word. The hard part comes in determining what is owed, how much is owed, and for how long. People with toxic guilt are not very good at arriving at balanced responses to those questions. That's because they want to think of themselves as good sons or daughters. When parents have needs and desires, or even when they are *perceived* by their dutiful children as having needs and desires, the children jump to the rescue. When adult children want to break free from their old patterns of accommodating their parents' every whim, they often feel trapped.

Mother Guilt

"Mother guilt" gets a section of its own because it is so widely experienced and discussed. Often, people feel controlled by their mothers because the guilt of displeasing them is too much to bear. The common attitude is "just grit your teeth, do what your mother wants, and get it over with." Unfortunately, resentment follows closely on the heels of mother guilt, creating a relationship of hostile dependence. It is helpful to understand how this distressing dynamic evolves.

Mothers are the cultural rule-makers and rule-keepers. It was your mother who made you wear a cap when it was cold and forced you to take a bath. She established your routines and rituals— when you went to bed, brushed your teeth, took a nap, and so on. Our mothers were also the ones who monitored everything we did: *be sure you wear clean underwear; you could be in a wreck and wind up in the hospital!* Our mothers held us accountable: *call me when you get there.* We learned that we should never go on a date with someone our mother would not approve of.

The idea of mother as rule-maker is reflected in the culture in many ways. My husband and I enjoy eating at a restaurant where a sign on the wall reads, "Your mother always told you to eat a good breakfast."

We internalize these rules as we grow up, and they help us make good decisions for ourselves. We come to understand that our mothers made the rules and enforced them for our own good; they had our best interests at heart. (What we usually don't learn is that our mothers' behavior was also motivated by the societal repercussions that would ensue if they *didn't* teach us the rules! They knew that if they failed, even slightly, they would quickly be placed in the "bad mother" category.)

In adulthood it sometimes feels as though our mothers are still watching us—monitoring our behavior and holding us accountable. We resent that feeling, but nonetheless we also feel we "owe" our mother for all she did for us. Therefore, the dynamic develops of being angry at one's mother for being intrusive while simultaneously needing her approval. It is important to note that since guilt associated with mothers is largely culturally motivated, *all* mothers are blamed for instilling it—whether they actually have or not.

People with healthy guilt value their mothers and take care to maintain a close connection with them; however, their mothers do not control their lives. This is because healthy separation and individuation has occurred. As they grew up, children with healthy guilt began to assert their independence and move into true adulthood.

People with toxic guilt about their mothers, on the other hand, never successfully moved out from under their mothers' control. This could be because the mother was unwilling to allow it, or because the child was particularly needy. The end result is that the mother's influence on the child remains excessive. When people with toxic guilt decide to claim true independence from their mothers—usually by doing something their mothers would not approve of—it can feel as if their very identities are at stake.

How Culture Influences Guilt About Children

In our culture, the way our children treat us is a measure of our worth. If they love us and respect us, we must have been good parents. If they don't, something must be wrong with us. For example, while his mother was alive, my husband's family gathered with other families at a little church cemetery on Memorial Day to decorate graves and have a covered-dish lunch. The church gave a prize to the family with the most people there.

The unspoken assumption was that the family with the most people attending had the best parents. As much as my husband and his siblings griped and complained every year about going, they wouldn't think of skipping the event and even insisted that their immediate family members attend. They knew their mother's identity and self-esteem were tied to their presence. For her, it was proof of her good mothering.

Our culture tells us that the way children turn out is also a reflection of their parents. If they turn out bad, they must have had bad parents. If they turn out well, their parents were good. For example, I went to high school with a boy who was popular and smart. He was from a prominent family in town. When the Vietnam War came along, my friend was drafted. During boot camp he had a mental breakdown and was discharged. Although he was quite impaired, his family hid his medical condition (schizophrenia) and pretended that nothing was wrong. His parents had been good parents, but it was clear that they felt their son's illness reflected poorly on them.

For the past twenty-five years, the divorce rate in our culture has been approximately 50 percent for all first marriages. Children of divorce grow up in two households; more often than not, the parents compete for their children's affection. Neither parent wants to be the bad guy and discipline the children because they fear loss of the children's affection. What if the child prefers the other parent because he or she is nicer and lets them do what they want?

Fear of not being loved, admired, or approved of by the child creates guilt. (Remember, if a parent is not loved by a child something must be wrong with the parent!) To avoid that guilt, the parent abdicates his or her role and does not discipline the child.

Parents who want to stop allowing their children to be in charge face a hefty dose of culturally imposed guilt. If parents decide to reclaim their authority, they must acknowledge that something has gone wrong. When parents institute discipline the kids will not like it, and the parents must face the guilt engendered by upsetting their children. If the children are older and the parents want to stop bailing them out of their predicaments, they must acknowledge that the kids have problems, leading to the guilty feeling that they must have been bad parents.

Religion and Guilt

Religious people are often more prone to toxic guilt than others. Many people who are not religious now, but were reared in families where a religious practice was observed, are also more vulnerable to toxic guilt. Religious tenets and practices learned during child-hood become so ingrained that even when they are rejected in adulthood, lingering ghosts remain. When religious people have trouble believing what they think they should believe, or fall short of their faith community's rules of proper conduct, they feel they have failed God and are less than good. Toxic guilt thrives in this environment.

Images of God and Toxic Guilt

When I have clients who know exactly what they need to do for themselves—get a divorce, have an abortion, cut the purse strings with a child, go against a parent's will, claim their sexuality, quit a job, get a job—but are immobilized by guilt, I often suspect that some religious prohibition is behind their paralysis. In the process of exploring their perspective on faith, I ask questions about their concept of God. The questions are: What or who is God to you? Where is God in your struggle? What does God say about this situation? Who are you to God?

The image people have of God greatly influences what they think about the nature of God, and what they think about the nature of God influences their vulnerability to toxic guilt. Although some traditions, Christianity included, believe no image or figure should be used to represent God, many people find relating to a formless, shapeless deity difficult. Therefore, most of us conjure up an image of God.

Do you picture God as a tall, stern-looking old man with a long white beard, dressed in a flowing white robe and surrounded by clouds? Does God look like your kindly grandfather, or maybe your mean old uncle? If God is watching you from a distance as the popular song suggests, what is God's attitude? Watching and judging? Watching and intervening? Watching and loving? Watching dispassionately and doing nothing?

It is difficult to imagine a genderless deity, but gender evokes certain stereotypes. If you think of God as male and you have had difficult or abusive relationships with males, it may be almost impossible for you to imagine God as a compassionate being. Indeed, the image of a male God may be so off-putting to some people that a relationship with God is out of the question. For example, if you are male and never measured up in the eyes of your father, are you able to feel you are good enough for God? If you are female, do you feel you are less important to God than a man because a man shares the gender of the Almighty?

A sense of not being good enough is the bedrock of toxic guilt; thus the image of God as masculine is enough to set some men up for a lifetime of guilt because of their relationship with their fathers, and to make some women feel guilty simply because they are female.

Victims of sexual abuse usually assume some responsibility for the abuse. Most feel that they were abused because something was bad or wrong about *them*. And since most perpetrators of sexual abuse are male, the image of a male God underscores the guilt of abuse for some people.

The Christian church's traditional language about and images of God emphasize God's masculinity, but according to scripture, feminine characteristics are also attributes of God. In recent years, feminist theologians and others have argued for equality of gender in referencing the divine. It has been an uphill battle; although characterizations of femininity in ancient cultures (and in a few contemporary ones) evoke wisdom and strength, characterizations of femininity in contemporary Western cultures generally evoke negative characteristics such as being weak, dependent, and manipulative. Many church officials and believers have strongly resisted the conceptualization of God as female, illustrating how deeply rooted the masculine ideal of God is in the collective consciousness of Christians (and perhaps in followers of other world religions).

When I was a campus minister, I did an exercise with my college students to help them explore the ways in which gender might influence their image of God. "If God were a woman," I said, "what would she look like?"

"She'd be big and soft like my grandmother," offered a spirited student with long chestnut hair. "She'd be baking and have on an apron all smudged with flour. She'd hug me, and when she did I'd notice her smell, like apples and cinnamon."

A thoughtful young woman in a hooded sweatshirt sitting next to her spoke next. "She'd be a gypsy. She'd wear brightly colored clothing and she'd dance, twirling 'round and 'round the campfire. Her jewelry would sparkle in the firelight and clink and jingle as she danced. She would be mysterious—a woman of mystery."

"Wrong!" The fellow with a goatee who was sprawled on a big floor pillow could barely contain himself. "She'd be a gorgeous blonde in high heels and a red dress." His snappy brown eyes danced. "No one could resist her. Now *that's* power!"

Each of these ideas suggests a different image of what God might be like. Maybe God is soft, warm, and accepting. Maybe God is a fiery mystery that intrigues but will always be beyond human comprehension. Or maybe God's power is fundamentally seductive, luring humankind into relationship like a sexy woman attracts a lover. As provocative as these images are, they are one-dimensional characterizations of the divine. Perhaps God's character is unlimited and much more complex. Perhaps God is multifaceted, like a diamond.

People with toxic guilt often think of God as rigid and one-dimensional. They see God as chronically displeased, a grumpy old man scanning the earth for souls who mess up; God is the rule-keeper in the sky that expects obedience and punishes wrong-doers. If you see God like this, no wonder you feel guilty all the time! People who see God as flexible and multidimensional may feel guilty when they fall short of what they think God wants and expects, but they are less apt to be consumed with toxic guilt because characteristics such as forgiveness, compassion, and understanding are incorporated into their image of God.

Race must also be considered in the discussion of images of God. If you are a person of color, pictures and statues of a Caucasian God can be off-putting. I once heard a pastor who was Asian and female talk about her struggle to overcome a distance she felt in her relationship with God. Then one night she dreamed of God as an Asian woman, like her mother. Suddenly, she felt the intimate connection to God that had eluded her for years.

Religious Fundamentalism and Toxic Guilt

Religious people want to please God. Following "God's law" or doing "God's will" is important. Defining just what that law or will means is a point of contention between various religions, as well as between differing groups within major religions.

Fundamentalists are those who understand the words of their tradition's holy writings in their most basic sense. What holy writing means to the devout is important because that understanding can fuel the fires of toxic guilt. Fundamentalism prescribes a highly structured approach to religion. Rules of godliness are precise, rigid, and strictly enforced. This creates an environment in which toxic guilt flourishes.

Although there is little consensus about the definition of biblical literalism among Christian scholars, there is a collective understanding on the part of the general public of what biblical fundamentalism means, and it can be summarized by a popular bumper sticker: *God said it. It's the Truth. That's the end of it.*

Christians who are not literalists understand the Bible differently than that. Non-literalists use various approaches in determining the meaning of scripture, including metaphor and allegory, historical setting, and intent of the author. Scholars also use collateral sources (documents from similar periods) to inform and enhance the study of Holy Scripture. These documents aid in the interpretation of terms, phrases, and stories found in the Bible, and ultimately help them understand God's message.

An example of the association between a literal interpretation of scripture and toxic guilt is evidenced by the many clients I have worked with who masturbate and feel guilty about it. Even though masturbation is widely practiced and understood in the wider culture, the rules against it are alive and well in some religious circles. The prohibition against the practice is purported to come from an Old Testament passage (Genesis 38:9–10). It is the story of a man named Onan. Onan's father commanded him to marry his dead brother's wife and impregnate her. Instead, Onan "spilled his seed on the ground." This was displeasing to the Lord, and the Lord slew him.

One does not really know why the Lord was displeased. Was it because Onan masturbated, or was it because he disobeyed his father, or was it because an heir was not produced for the deceased brother? Some religious authorities are all too happy to insist that masturbating was the sin. My clients have heard their pastors' admonishment against masturbation, and when they do self-gratify, the guilt is overwhelming. Being healthy sexual beings, they continue to masturbate; and being victims of their church's doctrine, they continue to feel guilty. This is difficult enough for males, but even worse for women, who historically have faced both religious and cultural prohibitions against masturbation.

Faith and Expectations

Failed expectations of what God could, would, or should do in the life of a believer cause some people to doubt, to be disappointed, or to disbelieve. Even worse, the believer whose expectations are not met often thinks the fault lies with him or her: *if I had been more faithful, a better person, more loving, or more giving, God would have acted in my favor.* This thinking is ideal soil for growing and cultivating toxic guilt.

Some people who are religious expect their faith to be so strong that they shouldn't question anything. When they do have doubts and questions, they feel guilty and think something about them is lacking. Even worse, they may feel that God is displeased with them because their faith is weak—and feel guilty about that.

Religion and Divorce

Most of the leading world religions, including Christianity, have prohibitions against divorce. Yet many, many people of faith are divorced or long to get divorced. Some divorced people feel guilty for years about having gone against their religious teachings, while others who long to escape their marriages stay trapped in them for the rest of their lives because the guilt of breaking the divorce prohibition is too much to bear.

If you are among the many religious people who are divorced, or who would like to be divorced, how do you reconcile the reality of your life with the dictates of your faith? I think it is helpful to compare the prohibition against divorce to your concept of God. If you understand God as a compassionate being who has no desire for people to be trapped, you may have some flexibility in the way you regard divorce.

If you are a Christian, you know that a great deal of the life of Christ was about liberating people from oppression of all types—including disease, death, and guilt. Oppression can also occur in relationships. When friendships go sour, business relationships fail, and love relationships fall apart, oppression is often at least part of the problem. Although one hopes for and expects much more in important and intimate relationships such as marriage, it doesn't always happen that way.

In the Christian tradition, among others, marriage is a commitment to be honored for life. But what if a marriage is characterized by unhappiness and oppression for one or both partners? I believe that when a marital relationship subjugates either partner, keeping him or her from being free to become fully and completely the person God created him or her to be, the rules change. I do not believe that God would continue to sanction a union that held any person hostage.

Faithful followers of most of the world's religions could probably agree that the essence of God is compassion. Divine compassion is so powerful, so sweet, so inclusive, and so abiding that we mortals cannot begin to comprehend it. Certainly, divine compassion is greater than yours or mine. Yet as flawed and imperfect as my compassion is, I love my children and want them to be happy and fulfilled in life. If my daughter or son was oppressed, dishonored, or just plain miserable in a marriage, and had done everything possible to salvage the relationship, I would give my permission—if not outright encouragement—for my child to leave the relationship. I could not, and do not, worship a God whose compassion is less than mine. I can't imagine a God who would place the marriage vow above the health and happiness of the human beings in the marriage.

Catholic Guilt

As I was working on this book I heard this comment over and over: "Guilt! Of course I have guilt—I'm a Catholic!" The connection between Catholicism and guilt seems universal. As I mentioned earlier, the more highly structured a religion, the more fertile the ground it provides for toxic guilt. My experience with several third-generation Roman Catholic clients illustrates this dynamic.

The immigrant ancestors of my clients brought a vibrant and highly structured faith to America along with their worldly possessions. Faithful attendance at mass on Sunday was not an option; it was a way of life. As generations passed and the culture around these families evolved, adherence to religious expectations did not change. Attendance at mass remained the family norm. When my clients' adult lifestyles did not reflect this important activity, a menacing sense of guilt festered in the depth of their beings. They did not need Papa's reprimands or Mama's pleadings; the voice within was enough.

When confronted with life's problems—a cheating spouse, a wayward child, chronic illness—fear and an immobilizing sense that they were somehow *bad* were the prevailing feelings. My clients could not see what was behind the distress they felt or understand why they were stuck in an emotional quagmire. Through therapy, the realization came that a subterranean guilt was lurking in their souls, whispering *It's all your fault. You were bad. You did not go to mass like you were supposed to. You did not follow the rules. God is displeased.*

The same creeping guilt may be experienced by Catholics who practice birth control, have abortions, send their children to public school, get a divorce, or marry outside the faith.

Jewish Guilt

Judaism is also associated with guilt. Most people are familiar with the stereotype of the "Jewish mother." Comedians (most of them Jewish) have become famous and wealthy by embellishing the characteristics of a guilt-inducing, overbearing, demanding mother. Jewish guilt is also known to motivate behavior that leads to academic achievement, financial success, and business acumen. "My son, the doctor" sums up the ideal of the Jewish family.

Jewish guilt may be tied to strong and highly structured tribal standards. Since Judaism is both a religion and a culture, identity as a Jew has double significance; and to a Jew, identity is everything. Persecuted throughout history, Jews have fought long and hard to maintain their uniqueness as a people. Preserving heritage, from the Exodus to the Holocaust, is a way of life. The song "Tradition" from the popular play and movie *Fiddler on the Roof* says it all—tradition is at the heart of Judaism. The story also illustrates the importance of keeping the tribe pure: Jews should only marry Jews, and when the main character's daughter marries outside the faith, she is ostracized from the family.

Jews with healthy guilt are able to respect their heritage and make independent choices, such as not practicing the faith or marrying a Gentile. How difficult it must be for Jews with toxic guilt who would like to venture beyond tribal standards!

Now you know the difference between healthy and unhealthy guilt. You can identify the people who control you by making you feel guilty, and you know why they can. You also understand how psychology and culture influence the formation of toxic guilt. In the next section, you will explore the eight common guilt-inducing situations and find out if you are trapped in any of these situations because of toxic guilt.

Many people are, or have been, trapped in one or more of these predicaments, each one of which presents a dilemma that can create emotional paralysis. In these situations, it often becomes impossible for people to make good decisions and act upon them because the guilt is just too overwhelming. People may fantasize about acting on their desires, but the follow-through is not forthcoming. The next section maps out the swamps and bogs, dry creek beds and dangerous bluffs where travelers on a guilt trip get stuck.

Part II

The Eight Situations

7

But I Can't Leave Him: He Needs Me!

Leaving a relationship is, for many people, a guilt trip through hell. The thought of hurting the other person keeps well-meaning partners in bad or dead relationships for far too long.

When You Want to Leave a Relationship

One of the most important and compassionate things I do in my work as a relationship coach is helping people get out of bad relationships. Although I hear about people who "cut and run when the going gets rough" or "bail out at the drop of a hat," I haven't worked with anyone like that yet. My clients agonize over leaving a relationship.

Sometimes pulling out of an important relationship evokes so much guilt that people stay when they shouldn't or don't want to. Tolerating the intolerable becomes a way of life. Fantasies about leaving fill their thoughts:

- If he'd just find someone else, have an affair—then I could get out.
- This is awful, but I find myself thinking about what I'd wear to his funeral. I imagine what it would look like. . . . If he died, I'd be free. Isn't that the worst?

- I constantly daydream about a life without her—like if she just disappeared, you know, became a missing person. . . .

If you are trapped in the wrong relationship, you may be risking your emotional and physical health. If your relationship is unsatisfactory, answer the following questions to get a picture of how it may be affecting your health status:

- Are you so unhappy in your relationship that you have felt "down," depressed, or hopeless for more than a few days?
- Have your eating habits changed?
- Have you lost or gained weight because you are not hungry, are eating more, or are eating more often?
- Are your sleeping patterns different?
- Do you find little interest or pleasure in doing things you once enjoyed?
- Do you feel tired and have low energy much of the time? (This is the most subtle and insidious symptom of depression.)
- Are you anxious?
- Do you worry a lot?
- Have you had a sudden feeling of anxiety or fear, during which your heart raced and you were short of breath?
- Do you drink more alcohol or use more drugs than you should?
- Do you have gastrointestinal problems that don't seem to have an organic cause, such as indigestion, constipation, or diarrhea?
- Do you have chronic disorders such as migraine headaches, chronic fatigue syndrome, fibromyalgia, or arthritis?
- Is your sex life less than satisfying?

If you answered yes to five or more of these questions, there is a very good chance that your relationship is jeopardizing your health. A number of factors can cause these symptoms, but if you know that your distress is in response to your primary relationship, then remaining in it may have serious consequences.

I can speak to this not only as a therapist who has seen clients suffer physically and emotionally by staying in the wrong relationship, but from personal experience. In my first marriage I was plagued by a variety of health issues. I can't say that my problematic relationship caused these maladies, but I can say that when I left the relationship my health improved dramatically.

Your spiritual health may also be at risk. When I ask my clients if it makes sense to remain in a relationship that is detrimental to their health, they usually say, "No, but . . ." The "but" often has to do with some real or perceived religious belief, requirement, or rule.

Evaluate the religious implications of leaving your relationship by answering the following questions:

- Do you think you will make God angry if you leave the relationship?
- Do you think God is holding you to your marriage vow?
- Do you think God will not forgive you if you leave the relationship?
- Do you think God will punish you if you leave the relationship?
- Do you have reason to believe that your pastor or church community will chastise you if you leave your relationship?

If you answered yes to two or more of these questions, you may be trapped in a relationship by toxic guilt that stems from religious reasons. I believe that if either partner in a marriage is prevented from becoming the person God intended them to be because of restrictions placed upon them by the relationship, God would surely condone the dissolution of the marriage.

This conviction comes from two sources: first, my understanding of God as merciful, loving, and compassionate; and second, my perception of God as a loving parent. If your child came to you for permission to leave a terrible relationship and explained that her spirit was being crushed, that she had lost herself completely, that there was no joy left in life, and that grief and unhappiness characterized the relationship, what would you say? I think you would tell her to leave and give her your blessings. If you, an imperfect human parent, would not hesitate to grant your child her freedom, would not God, the perfect parent, do the same?

Although religious taboos about divorce may be the biggest reason why people stay in the wrong marriage, cultural baggage also plays a major role. No one wants to be perceived as a loser, and people with a history of failed relationships are portrayed as losers in popular fiction, in movies, and in the media. Better to stay in a bad relationship than experience the guilt of being a loser.

If children are involved, there is another cultural prohibition against leaving a relationship. The partner who leaves is blamed for "splitting up the family." He or she is accused of being selfish for not "putting the children first." Nothing is more guilt-inducing than the thought that *you* are to blame for your children's pain.

Both religious and cultural consciousness support the myth that it is never OK to hurt another person, especially a spouse. Many people stay in the wrong relationship because the guilt of hurting someone they once loved is too much to bear.

Another religious and cultural prohibition against leaving a committed relationship is the perceived sanctity of the marriage vows. Making a promise to God and giving your word to another in front of witnesses is inviolable to many people. They take their vows so seriously that the thought of breaking them evokes overwhelming guilt.

And last, but certainly not least, is the notion that God forbid we ever leave someone who *needs* us. It's almost as if need is the glue that keeps some couples together and keeps people stuck in bad relationships. People could drown in the guilt that floods through them when they think about leaving someone who needs them.

Here is a way to think about marital vows, or other promises and commitments made to a partner, that has been helpful to many people. As a therapist and relationship coach, I work both with individuals and with couples. An individual is an entity, and when I do individual therapy, my focus, attention, and suggestions relate to that particular person. When I work with a couple, there are two people to consider, but there is also a third presence. The *relationship* is also an entity with a life of its own.

Each partner in the couple can be relatively healthy and high-functioning, while the relationship of the two together can be quite sick indeed. Sometimes the relationship is in such poor health that it dies. Perhaps "until death do us part" means *I promise my love and loyalty until I die, you die, or our relationship dies.* Using that model, if the relationship is dead, the obligation has been met and the vows have been honored.

It might be a good idea to seek the help of a professional therapist or counselor before you leave an important relationship, especially if you are not sure how you really feel or what you really want to do. A good therapist will create a safe environment and push the envelope at the same time. You will find out if there's something worth saving, or if it's time to cut your losses and move on.

My happiest experience as a coach is to watch a couple discover or rediscover each other in the course of therapy. Unfortunately, that is not always the case—usually because it is too little, too late for one of the partners. When that is the case, I do my best to help the couple dissolve their union with compassion and respect for each other.

Nelson's Story

Nelson's story is a good example of how staying in a bad marriage can exact a price on a person's health and well-being. It also serves to illustrate the insidious power of guilt.

Nelson was living a life of quiet desperation. His wife was demanding and negative. Nothing he did pleased her, and whatever he did was never enough. This caused him such anguish that he could hardly concentrate at work. His blood pressure had been going up and his doctor was concerned. Things he once enjoyed, like occasional golf or tennis or weekly basketball games at the gym, had lost their appeal. He had no energy anymore and only slept two or three hours a night.

When I met Nelson in the lobby of my office, I thought he was attractive and fit in a "he must run or bike" sort of way. I escorted him to my therapy room, and after he settled himself on the sofa across from me, he began telling me about his life. He was a forty-two-year-old CPA and worked in a small firm that provided service to an affluent clientele. He was married to Beth and had two children, ages seven and nine. He was the treasurer of his country club and had a position of responsibility in his church. His wife played tennis, was active in the PTA, and belonged to a book club. The family lived in a prestigious neighborhood. Everyone thought he had it all.

He sank back into my sofa with a heavy sigh. "I met Beth in grad school. She was smart, funny, and career-minded—everything I wanted. It all changed after we got married. She worked less than a year and then quit—some career!" He shook his head and went on. "She wanted a house. She wanted children. We bought an older home, but the restoration and redecorating became an endless nightmare. She was never satisfied. We had children, but that didn't make her happy either." Exhaling noisily, he leaned on his knees and stared into his hands. "This is hard for me. I'm not one to complain, especially about my wife! It makes me feel—I don't know—like I'm breaking the rules."

I waited.

"Then she wanted a bigger house, a new one this time. We got one, of course. I can't keep up with her—she spends money faster than I can make it. The house is a mess and she won't cook. We go out to dinner at least four times a week. She couldn't care less about anything I'm interested in. We have nothing in common anymore." He put his head in his hands and ran his fingers through his hair nervously. "We haven't had sex for over a year, and frankly, at this point, I don't care. She's irritated and angry with me most of the time. I can't take much more. . . ."

"How long have you been this miserable?"

"About three years."

"Are you open to doing marital therapy with your wife?"

Nelson rested his chin in his hands and stared at the floor in front of him for a minute. He looked up. "It's worth a try—I'd do about anything to make this thing work."

For the next four months I met with Nelson and Beth on a weekly basis. Beth was a beautiful, intelligent woman, but unfortunately was as demanding and critical as Nelson had described. In what was to be our final session, Beth lambasted Nelson for being less than attentive at a dinner party the night before. She accused him of deserting her while he socialized with others.

"I can't babysit you every time we go to a party, Beth," he said. "You know all those people—they're your friends too. You have to learn to stand on your own two feet." Beth glared at him, and then she stormed out of the office without a word.

Nelson's face was a picture of resignation. "That's it. I can't do this anymore."

We spent the remainder of the hour reviewing the progress, or lack thereof, of the marital work. Nelson admitted that try as he would, he could not reclaim any feelings of love for his wife.

"Are you going to end the relationship?" I asked.

Nelson visibly paled. "You mean divorce?"

"Yes."

Now he looked really ill. "I don't know if I could do it."

"Why not?"

"The guilt."

Analyzing Nelson's Guilt

Toxic guilt was keeping Nelson trapped in a miserable marriage. Although he was drowning in unhappiness and despair, the thought of divorce made him physically ill. In Nelson's world, divorce was against all the rules. He was a responsible person, a leader in his church and community. He valued the good opinion of others, which he had worked so hard to achieve. Beth needed him, both emotionally and financially, and he took care of everything. What would she do without him? How could he break his marital vows, split up his family, and still live with himself?

Nelson found answers to these questions as he worked through the five steps that begin in Chapter 15. Although toxic guilt deceived him into believing there was no way out, Nelson discovered that it *was* possible to leave the relationship and still be able to see himself as a good man. Ultimately, he filed for divorce.

Toxic guilt keeps people trapped in marriages and plays a leading role in contentious, destructive divorces. Too guilty to leave relationships that suck the life out of them, people slowly die of emotional starvation.

The most common cause of divorce is involvement with a third party, and I understand why. It is human nature to reach for food when you are hungry, and it is just as natural to reach out when someone offers emotional nourishment if you haven't had any for a long time. Finding someone else can feel like rebirth and is often the catalyst that brings a marriage to an end. Unfortunately, the end is usually an explosion.

If toxic guilt were not so powerful, an unhappy spouse could look her partner in the eyes and tell the truth: "I'm sorry, but I don't love you anymore. I wish I did, but I don't. For me, this marriage is over." But alas, most people are too guilty to take such an honest stand, and so cheating, betrayal, and deception become the path of least resistance.

If you are trapped in a relationship because of toxic guilt, read on. Escape is possible. I will show you how to overcome guilt so that you can get out with dignity, integrity, and compassion.

8

But They're My Children!

There are parents whose entire world revolves around their children. After all, the parents believe, it's all their fault if their children don't grow up to be exemplary citizens. The children's interests, activities, homework, athletics, and friends reign supreme over everything else in the parents' lives.

I'm not talking about responsible parents who are involved, attentive, and loving. I'm talking about parents whose lives are unbalanced. The attention and energy spent on these kids is ridiculous.

Are Your Children Running Your Life?

Here are some questions to ask yourself to determine if you are, in fact, trapped by guilt over your children:

- Do you feel anxious, nervous, or upset because your child is not interested in what you want him to be interested in? (For example: piano lessons, basketball, history, biology, a particular career, and so on.)
- Do you "lobby" your child in an attempt to interest her in activities or academics that you feel are important, even when it is clear your child does not feel that way?
- Do you feel anxious, nervous, or upset when your child has a fight with his girlfriend or boyfriend?

- Do you go through your child's backpack, read her journal, check her text messages, or listen to her phone conversations when there is no real reason to? (A real reason would be the possibility of criminal activity, risk for self-harm, and so on.)
- If your child is away from home (for visitation with the other parent, college, summer camp, and so on), do you call one or more times per day?
- Do you always side with your child against authority figures? (For example: police, teachers, principals, employers, and so on.)
- Would you take it personally and be upset if your child chose a college that was not the one you wanted him to attend?
- If you institute a consequence for bad behavior (such as a time-out; the loss of computer, car, or allowance; being grounded; and so on), do you usually go back on it?
- Assuming your child is not an infant or toddler, do her activities and wishes usually take precedence over yours?
- Are all your friends connected to your child in some way? (For example: parents of your child's peers; people who teach, coach, or mentor your child; and so on.)
- Are you involved in all your child's activities? (If you coach his soccer team, are homeroom mother, teach his Sunday school class, and participate in his ballet lessons, the answer is yes.)
- Are you married with a child who is an adolescent or older, but still consider your child the most important person in your life?
- Do you do homework assignments for your child?
- Does your child have unlimited access to your home and possessions?
- Do you consider your child your best friend?
- Does your child frequently talk you into changing the rules? (For example: curfew time, access to the car, homework rules, requirements to notify you of her whereabouts, and so on.)

- If your child had an argument with a friend and was upset, would you intervene by talking with the friend yourself?
- Do you buy your child unnecessary items when you don't really have the money to do it?
- For divorced parents only: have you been avoiding going on dates because you do not want to upset the children?
- For divorced parents only: do you have a significant other but hide the relationship from your child because you do not want to upset him?

If you answered yes to four or more questions, it's likely that you have an unresolved guilt issue with your child. There are two major sources of this kind of guilt: parent overinvolvement and parent underinvolvement. However, it may be that you were a good enough parent; that is, you were appropriately attentive and loving and your discipline was balanced, but your children still did not turn out to be the loving, respectful, responsible, happy, and fulfilled individuals you wanted them to be.

Sometimes one of the hardest things for parents to realize is that they are not as powerful in the lives of their children as they thought. Kids are who they are right from birth, and they are different from their parents. But some guilt-ridden parents take the blame anyway. The next part of this chapter will explore the reasons why many parents blame themselves for their children's situation.

Parent Overinvolvement

There are all sorts of reasons for parents to be overinvolved in their children's lives, and guilt is behind most of them. Stay-at-home moms may feel guilty for not putting their education to good use, or for not contributing to the family finances, or both. They may feel obliged to become "supermoms" as a way to justify their unemployed status. They may throw themselves into their kids' lives as a way to make peace with their own. Sound crazy? It's not crazy, just out of balance and uninformed. It's out of balance because moms like these do not devote enough time and energy to their own growth and interests. It is uninformed because they do not seem to know that kids need to learn their place in the world. How does one teach children that the world does not revolve around them if, indeed, it does? (Of course, not all stay-at-home moms are caught in the supermom syndrome, but many are and suffer because of it.)

Some parents become overinvolved in their children's lives because they did not have happy childhoods themselves. Perhaps they were not successful in school—academically, athletically, or socially—and feel guilty about being failures. Now that they have the opportunity to make up for their shortcomings through their children, they pressure their kids to succeed and are overinvolved in their lives.

Conversely, there are parents who were quite successful as children and would feel like failures (and therefore guilty) if their children did not follow suit. They, too, become overinvolved and pressure their kids to succeed.

Some parents are overinvolved in the lives of their children because they don't have lives of their own. Instead of having their own interests, activities, and social contacts, they turn to their children to get these needs met.

Parental overinvolvement is often a fallout of divorce. Both parents—and in particular, the one who instigated the divorce—may feel guilty about disrupting their child's world. They feel guilty about the pain and loss they have caused, so they overindulge their child—lavishing attention, affection, and material goods on him or her without benefit of discipline and limit-setting. Before long, these children learn to manipulate and control their parents, playing them off of each other in order to get what they want.

Many times, when both parents work, they feel guilty that they spend so little time with their children, and so they want the time spent together to be as easy and guilt-free as possible. As a result, they are sometimes loath to "waste" that time nagging their children about chores or rules and instead let those things slide, going overboard on praise and not following through on discipline.

When parents fail to hold children accountable for their behavior or fail to teach them to be responsible, there are predictable outcomes. The kids become self-centered and demanding, and the parents wind up anxiously waiting for their children to become better citizens.

Conflict about the laundry, oddly enough, makes a good example of how guilt-ridden parents can improve their lives and the lives of their children. (Laundry and the kids are the focus of more therapy sessions than most people would guess!) The reality that children can do laundry somehow escapes well-intentioned parents. It's a small thing, or maybe not. Like a grain of sand in an oyster, a small irritation can grow into something much larger. The following story illustrates a typical scenario.

The Turner Family Story

In the Turner family, twelve-year-old Billy refuses to put his dirty clothes in the hamper. Samantha, his fourteen-year-old sister, has tantrums if her favorite jeans haven't been laundered. Mom's physically exhausted and emotionally drained because she works outside the home as well as in it and feels guilty about not being more available to the children. Dad, who works even longer hours than Mom does, can't understand why his wife is so ill-tempered lately. She goes into tirades about the kids when he comes home from work, and she's not very nice to him either. So they wind up in my office for couples coaching, angry and frustrated with each other. They begin by describing the ongoing conflict about the laundry.

"Why are you doing a fourteen-year-old adolescent's laundry?" is my first question.

The parents look at each other, dumbfounded.

"Aren't I supposed to?" says Mom.

She looks to Dad for answers, and he looks back. Silence. He thinks she's supposed to too.

About this time I suggest that Mom might be feeling guilty because she is not able to hold down a job and still do everything her mother (who did not work outside the home) did. Mom lights up like a Christmas tree because somebody gets it, and after a short discussion Dad gets it too. They quickly grasp the concept that Mom's guilt is out of proportion to the situation. They are aware that both parents work outside the home in most families these days, and they acknowledge that children are not necessarily damaged emotionally because of it.

Mom decides she sure could use some help from her able-bodied, age-appropriate offspring, and Dad is surprised he didn't think of it. It does not take long for Mr. and Mrs. Turner to see that if they make their children responsible and stop trying to take on everything themselves out of guilt, life for everyone would be better.

The couple leave my office with a plan: they will teach Billy and Samantha how to do their own laundry, and Mom will resign as head laundress. This actually lets Mom and Dad off the hook because when Billy and Samantha are responsible for their own laundry, there is no one to blame but themselves when all their clothes are dirty or the favorite jeans aren't ready. Better yet, the parents have no reason to feel guilty about it.

Parental Underinvolvement

Parents who believe they have neglected their children often feel so guilty about it that they spend the rest of their lives in bondage to them. I am not talking about parents with criminal minds who willfully neglect their children and put them in danger both emotionally and physically, because they may feel very little guilt. I am talking about those parents whose lives were so chaotic when their children were young that they could not be as involved as they wanted to be. Some examples are parents who had alcoholic, disabled, or very ill spouses or parents who were alcoholic, disabled, or very ill themselves; parents who had to work more than one job just to make ends meet; single parents shouldering all the responsibility of the family; and parents who were caregivers to ill or aged family members.

Through no fault of their own, these parents are not usually able to be as involved in their children's lives as they might wish. Toxic guilt gets a foothold, and when the children are older and the parents' lives more settled, the parents try to make it up to the kids—often in unreasonable ways and for far too long. Such was the case in Joanna's story.

Joanna's Story

Joanna fell apart when her boys were young. A single mother at the time, overworked and going through her own deep emotional waters, she simply couldn't manage any longer. She gave custody of the boys over to their father and moved to her sister's home in another state. While living with her sister she went to therapy, started taking medication, and eventually got better; it took two years. Feeling stronger and longing for her children, Joanna moved back. She was involved in her boys' lives, but they continued to live with their father.

The boys began to run amok during their teenage years: truancy, alcohol, drugs, the whole nine yards. Joanna, determined to make up for the lost years, turned her full attention to her sons. From ages fifteen and seventeen to their late twenties and early thirties, they owned her. She felt so guilty for having left them as children that she couldn't say no to them. She knew better, but in the marrow of her bones were those old mother-blaming messages, which overrode intellect and reason.

Although Joanna had done the best she could when the boys were young and she was ill, in some deep place in her heart she felt responsible for her sons' bad choices. It was all her fault. You can guess the outcome of that: she bought houses for them, bailed them out of jail, moved them in with her, and gave them money. The only thing that changed was that her emotional health suffered. At one point not too long ago, she said she'd been thinking about leaving the state and moving back to her sister's.

Analyzing Joanna's Guilt

Joanna felt guilty for abandoning her children when they were young. Although she did the best she could do at the time, she knew her parenting was dismal. This healthy guilt motivated her to do all she could to be a good parent when she recovered. Although she did not have custody of her boys, she saw them as often as she could. They visited her home every week, and she attended all the school and extracurricular activities that she possibly could. She supported her children financially and emotionally.

But toxic guilt took over. Instead of setting reasonable limits on what she would and would not do for her boys, she was at their beck and call. But no matter what she did for them, their behavior did not change. The result of toxic guilt was that Joanna overindulged her children and depleted her financial and emotional resources.

Parents Who Are Good Enough

Even when people love, honor, and respect their children and discipline them appropriately, there is no guarantee that the children will grow up to be good citizens who lead meaningful and satisfying lives. These are the parents who watch helplessly as their children spiral downward. They blame themselves for what their children are becoming, when there really is nothing they could have done that would have made a difference.

Juan's parents stood by helplessly and watched their bright, happy fifth-grade boy morph into a surly, smart-mouthed teen who hangs out with a bunch of losers, sleeps through classes, and skips school.

Jenny's parents grieve that what was once their sweet, bubbly little ballet dancer now dresses gothic, has a tongue piercing, and steals money from her mom's purse.

Eddie went off to college, partied his way out, and came home to roost. Now he doesn't go to school or have a job. He's out all night with old high-school buddies, sleeps until noon, and storms out of the house when Mom or Dad confronts him about his behavior.

Suzy flunked out of State U. Now she lives with a man who doesn't have a job. Her parents are terrified she'll get pregnant. They have no idea how she could she support a child on her salary as a telemarketer.

Some parents worry because their children do not seem to have healthy relationships. They choose partners who are all wrong and hang on to them in spite of the chaos and craziness. Others agonize over children who sink into substance abuse or depression, or make disastrous financial mistakes—running up credit card debts, loaning money to irresponsible friends, making major purchases they can't afford, or getting in trouble for writing bounced checks.

Parents who watch their children make terrible choices are always grief-stricken and usually guilt-ridden. They ask: *What did we do? Where did we go wrong?* By the time I see parents like these they've tried everything—made demands, threatened, supported their children emotionally and financially, encouraged, cajoled, and prayed—but nothing's worked. They sit in my office stunned and worried. What should they do?

When parents are bound and determined to blame themselves for their adult children's problems, and feel responsible to somehow fix their lives or make it up to them, the outcome is predictably dismal. The children are overindulged but do not improve, and the parents are so focused on them that their own lives suffer.

If toxic guilt has a grip on you and you blame yourself for your children's problems, it is not too late. You can get your life back by following the five steps coming up. You may not be able to change your children, although they may change in response to your new behavior. But whatever goes on with them, you deserve to be free.

9

Yes, Mom, of Course I'll Do It

Although it is a good thing when people are loving, respectful, compassionate sons or daughters, it is not a good thing when children feel entirely responsible for their parents' well-being. People who believe that the happiness, health, sobriety, or financial security of their parents is solely their responsibility are trapped. They are not free to live their own lives; they become so guilty when their parents are in distress of any kind that they either drop everything to rush and fix the problem, or worry and fret, or both.

Usually, people who abdicate their lives to their parents in this way are overly concerned about being good sons or daughters. Many have the "perfect child syndrome," believing that if they could be a perfect son or daughter, all would be well with Mom and Dad.

If this strikes a chord with you, it may be important to explore your understanding of what a "good" son or daughter is.

Are You Indentured to Your Parents?

Answer the following questions to see if your need to please your parents might be motivated by toxic guilt.

- Do you drop whatever it is you are doing if a parent needs something?

- Do you feel compelled to call your parents every day when you are on vacation?
- If a parent seems anxious, upset, or depressed, do you in turn feel anxious, upset, or depressed?
- If your parents have a problem, do you feel compelled to try to solve it?
- Are you the go-between when your parents are in conflict?
- Would you leave a love relationship if your parents did not approve?
- Are you willing to do something that you want to do (for example: get a divorce, get married, have a baby, pursue a career, move, take a trip) if your parents object?
- Do your parents' needs or wishes take precedence over the needs or wishes of your spouse?
- Do you include your parents in family vacations even when you'd rather not?
- Does your parents' schedule take precedence when you have something else planned? (For example, you cancel an event with friends if your parents invite you to their house.)
- Is there competition between you and your siblings for your parents' favor?
- Would you (or did you) attend the college or university of your parents' choice, even if you had another preference?
- Would you join an organization (sorority, fraternity, country club, social club, civic club, and so on) solely because your parents wanted you to?
- Do you need your parents' approval in order to make major purchases?
- Are you bound by your parents' religious preference? (That is, you would not become a member of another faith community or stop religious practice completely even if you wanted to.)

- Do you lie to your parents about who you are? (For example, if you are gay or lesbian, Democrat or Republican, and so on, and don't want them to know.)
- Do you lie to your parents about what you do? (For example, dance, drink alcohol, gamble, and so on.)

If you answered yes to four or more of these questions, toxic guilt may be dictating your relationship with your parents and robbing you of independence.

Often, people who are indentured to their parents have never outgrown an intense need for their parents' approval. When their parents are displeased with them it is almost intolerable: guilt floods their emotional reservoirs and drowns their self-worth. They will do almost anything to please their parents.

Aspiring to be a good son or daughter is a noble endeavor—but believing that if you just try hard enough you will win your parents' approval, when you never had it in the first place, is a doomed expectation. Believing that you can make your parents happy is a recipe for failure, and allowing your parents to run your life is a tragedy.

If you feel controlled by your parents, the trouble may come partially from the way you were raised. Strange as it may seem, if you were either neglected or overindulged by your parents as a child, you may be overly dependent on them as an adult.

Children of neglectful parents live the notion that something is bad or wrong about them. They believe that if they were just good enough, smart enough, pretty enough, successful enough, and so on, their parents would love them. They spend their lives driven by the need to win their parents' approval.

As I mentioned in Chapter 8, parents of overindulged children hamper their children's developing independence. These parents often fail to discipline their children, and they run interference in their children's lives much too often and for much too long.

There are a number of reasons why parents fail to discipline and become overinvolved. Some parents may be afraid that their children will not love them if they do not give them what they want. Others may be trying to justify their stay-at-home status. There are those who may be trying to live the life they never had through their children. Some may be trying to bolster their own fragile self-image through their children's accomplishments. And some may be trying to make up for all they didn't get from their own parents as children.

The stereotype of the stage mother or sports father depicts the parenting style of the overinvolved, overindulgent parent. The children of these parents often feel guilty if they don't "pay their parents back" for all their sacrifices.

Chip's Story

Chip attended college at his father's alma mater. Although the college was miles from his hometown, his father was so involved in his life that Chip might as well have been living at home. His father phoned several times every day, and was hurt and upset if his son was unavailable and did not return the calls right away.

When they talked, Chip felt interrogated; his father wanted to know everything—what he was doing, where he was going, and with whom. He wanted a running account of grades and athletic activities. Chip's father made sure his son joined the fraternity he was in during college. Actually, Chip was only minimally interested in attending college in the first place and had not been interested in joining a fraternity at all. However, his father pressured Chip to do what he thought was important, and Chip wanted to please his father.

Chip was an unhappy young man. He wanted out—out of the fraternity, out of college, and out from under his father's thumb. He longed to take some time off, get a job, and live in the real world for a while, but he was trapped by guilt. He knew his father would be hurt, and Chip was tortured by the thought of letting him down. How could he take this step and follow his dream when it would mean disappointing his father?

Analyzing Chip's Guilt

Chip is like many adolescents and young adults whose need to please a parent charts the course for their lives. Chip knew his father wanted only the best for him, and he felt guilty for not being more appreciative. But more than that, the thought of disappointing his father was paralyzing. It was time for Chip to define himself, but toxic guilt was robbing him of the freedom to do it.

It is difficult for many young people to garner the strength to stand up to well-meaning but overinvolved parents, especially when the parents are paying their way through college! So instead of finding their own voices, they allow circumstances to speak for them. Such was the case with Chip. The guilt that rolled in when Chip contemplated talking to his father about what *he* wanted was overwhelming. So, he simply stopped going to class and eventually flunked out of college. He got what he wanted—independence— but at a high price.

If parents could only learn to step back and give their children room to find themselves, stories like Chip's would have a different ending. There are worse endings; suicide attempts and antisocial behavior (cheating, stealing, sexual aggression, and worse) can be tragic escapes for children who feel indentured to their parents.

Ellen's Story

Intrusive mothering can be equally problematic. I once worked with a young couple on the brink of divorce. Ellen was strikingly beautiful, a beauty-pageant winner since childhood. Talented as well, she had gone on to become a finalist in more than one national contest. Her mother was very much a part of her daughter's activities from the beginning—enrolling her in dance classes, entering her in pageants, traveling with her to contests, and coaching her all the way. Mother and daughter were inseparable.

Nothing much changed when Ellen married Jeff; Ellen's mother was right in the middle of their relationship. When Ellen became pregnant, her mother was involved in every aspect of her daughter's pregnancy and delivery. After the baby was born, she advised the couple about child care whether they asked or not.

Ellen's relationship with her mother was the central conflict in her marriage. Jeff was sick and tired of her mother's intrusive behavior, but Ellen would not, or could not, stand up to her mother and put an end to it.

When Jeff and Ellen came to me for couples' therapy, they were on the brink of divorce. In one intense session, Jeff turned to me and said, "Do you think it's OK that my wife sleeps in bed with her mother instead of with me when we visit?"

I explored the situation with Ellen and learned that she was terrified of disappointing her mother in any way. Ellen wanted a separate, private life with Jeff, but if she put even the slightest distance between herself and her mother, there was hell to pay; her mother would withdraw, sulk, and make innuendoes about Ellen being ungrateful. Ellen would feel terribly guilty in response because, after all, her mother had devoted her whole life to Ellen. Sleeping with her mother was a way to assure her mother of her continued importance in Ellen's life, but this guilt-induced behavior was unacceptable to her baffled and confused husband. Ellen's attempt to please her mother was about to cost her a marriage.

Analyzing Ellen's Guilt

Ellen felt she owed her mother everything; it's not an uncommon assumption. Mother guilt runs deep in the human psyche and is fueled by psychological, religious, social, and cultural tenets. In Ellen's case, the psychological roots of toxic guilt were planted by her mother's overinvolvement and self-sacrifice. A religious emphasis on honoring one's parents and the sanctity of motherhood also fueled Ellen's guilt. With all these forces in play, Ellen felt so guilty that she could not deny her mother anything, even when it put her marriage in jeopardy.

Gloria's Story

Gloria was an amazing woman. Her childhood family had been so chaotic that her five siblings were, one by one, removed from the home and placed in foster care—except for Gloria. Although she was the "good" one, her mother's interest and energy was devoted to her wayward siblings.

Against all odds, Gloria succeeded in school, stayed away from alcohol and drugs, and did not get into trouble. She graduated from high school and joined the army. When she completed active duty, the army paid her way through nursing school.

I saw her in therapy for several years. The situations and issues changed, but the dynamics were always the same. She organized her life around trying to please her mother. When her errant siblings wound up in jail or ran out of money, Gloria's mother pressured her to bail them out and take them in. All of Gloria's free time was spent managing the lives of her siblings. She babysat their children, arranged legal aid for them, and carted them to and fro.

Her dysfunctional family controlled her. There was nothing left of Gloria for Gloria. It was no surprise that she was anxious, depressed, and had multiple health problems.

Analyzing Gloria's Guilt

Gloria's mother ran her life, and Gloria allowed it. She was consumed by guilt and driven by her need for her mother's approval. Since her mother's affection and attention were lavished on her siblings, Gloria felt there must be something terribly wrong with *her*. Gloria felt entirely responsible for her mother's happiness and guilty about her mother's difficult life. She also felt guilty that she had escaped repeating it.

Gloria, and people like her, long for a close relationship with their parents—and no matter how many times they are disappointed, they live with the hope that they can make it happen. They are also racked by guilt: *What did I do to make my mom and dad treat me this way? What is wrong about me?* Feeling guilty because they never seem to get it right for their parents, they are driven to try and please them.

Others dance to their parents' tune because they feel they owe them. It is important to honor your parents, but it is not reasonable to believe you owe your life to them just because they gave birth to you.

If you are controlled by the need to please your parents, toxic guilt is the driving force. The five steps coming up will teach you how to escape this trap and live life on your own terms.

10

But God Will Strike
Me Down if I Don't

Unfortunately, institutional religion is just that: an institution. It is not immune to corruption. There are healthy and unhealthy faith traditions, and there are healthy and unhealthy religious communities. Unhealthy religious groups demean and virtually enslave their members, rather than supporting and liberating them. Religious abuse is a reality, and the guilt induced by some of these communities is toxic.

Healthy religious groups, on the other hand, encourage and support their members and promote independent thinking. But even so, guilt-inducing tenets and teachings can lurk below the surface. Often, these messages are the result of religious tradition rather than doctrine.

For example, most Christians believe that certain sins lead to eternal damnation. However, the doctrine of universal salvation (also called universal reconciliation), which has been part of Christianity since its very early days, is not commonly known. This doctrine supports the belief that all persons will be reconciled to God at some point, even if it is after death; all will be "saved."

This view is not generally part of Christian consciousness. What *is* in the forefront of Christian thinking is that you must do X, Y, or Z or you will go to hell for sure. If that isn't guilt-inducing, I don't know what is.

Historically, Jews have been plagued by prejudice and persecution. It is difficult to maintain a positive feeling about who you are when so many have been telling you there's something wrong with you for so long. The overarching sense of guilt that many Jews experience is understandable in that context.

Also, Jews grow up with stories about the suffering of their people throughout the ages. Accounts of the Holocaust are especially soul-searing. Contemporary Jews may feel guilty for feeling and expressing the sorrow and pain of their own lives, when it pales in light of the extreme and lengthy suffering of so many in the Holocaust.

Additionally, Jews are charged to "repair the world" (a concept known as *tikkun olam* in Hebrew), particularly through acts of social justice. This noble but formidable task can lead to a sense of guilt about not doing enough, or not being good enough to get the job done.

Unfortunately, I can't address other world religions because I simply don't know much about them, although I wish I did. I would not be surprised if Muslims, Hindus, and others also struggle with toxic guilt related to their faith. It does appear that the struggle between ancient religious teachings and contemporary life is universal. If you are from another world religion, you may find that the ideas discussed here will apply to you as well.

It is crucial to understand toxic guilt in relation to your particular religious community, because that is what impacts your life on a daily basis. To get a sense of whether you might be in an unhealthy religious community, take the following quiz:

Is Your Faith Tradition or Religious Community a Source of Toxic Guilt?

Answer the following questions to see if your faith tradition or religious community could be causing toxic guilt in your life:

- Do you belong to a faith tradition that forbids certain activities (drinking alcohol, dancing, viewing certain movies, having sex before marriage, and so on), but you routinely do those things anyway?
- Are you staying in a love relationship (marriage or otherwise) because you think God and/or your religious community would be displeased if you left?
- Do you go to religious services when you really don't want to because you're afraid you'll be judged harshly if you are absent?
- If you got a divorce, would you quit going to church, temple, or prayer meeting because it would be too humiliating to attend services?
- Do you refrain from asking questions that you would like to ask about your spirituality when you're with others from your religious community?
- Are you afraid that if members of your religious community really knew you, they would not associate with you anymore?
- If you were about to enter the liquor store and saw a member of your church nearby, would you turn around and go the other way?
- If you were on a date with a person your religious community would not approve of (such as someone of a different race or religious affiliation, or someone of the same gender), would you try to hide?

- If your opinions differ from those of other people in your religious community, do you keep them to yourself rather than expressing them?
- Do you feel you could never leave your religious community, even if you wanted to?
- Do you believe that God will love you only if you follow certain rules?
- Would you be shunned by members of your religious community if you had a misfortune other than loss, illness, or death? (For example: getting divorced, being convicted of a crime, being caught cheating on a spouse, having an alcohol or drug addiction, and so on.)
- Are you afraid to have political views that differ from those that prevail in your religious community?
- Would you be afraid to marry someone outside your faith tradition because your religious community would no longer accept you?

If you answered yes to three or more questions, toxic guilt could be holding you captive through your faith tradition or religious community.

You might remember from Chapter 4 that in order to have a healthy sense of self, it is crucial to be able to think of yourself as "good" or "right." Religious people want to please God by living the right way and being good. Faith traditions teach their followers how to do this by defining what God wants and expects. Rules for acceptable behavior and correct belief form the doctrine of each faith tradition.

Faith traditions that welcome questions, allow for uncertainty, and are not preoccupied with rules of proper conduct and correct belief are less likely to cultivate toxic guilt in their members than others. Faith traditions that reject uncertainty, focusing on specific rules of conduct and concrete belief requirements, create environments that are ripe for toxic guilt. That's because the more difficult it is to follow the prescribed rules and believe the correct things, the higher the risk for failure.

Guilt rushes in when people think they've failed. For example, if your religious community teaches that it is a sin to drink alcohol and you drink alcohol anyway, guilt is bound to be lurking somewhere. The same is true if you date someone from another religion, have sex before marriage, look at "dirty" magazines, dance, or do any number of things that your religious tradition teaches are wrong, bad, unholy, or sinful.

This is not to say that rules of conduct and correct beliefs are not important or desirable in a religious tradition; indeed, they are. But when they are seen as more important than compassion for self and others, something is askew. If you are in a religious community that places rules above love, it may be time to break free.

Implications of Breaking Free

If following the rules and believing what your religious community stipulates is more than you can do, it is likely that you will be besieged with toxic guilt. Constantly holding yourself to standards that you can't (or don't want to) live up to will make you feel terrible about yourself—it may even cause you to doubt your worth in the eyes of God.

If the teachings and tenets of your faith tradition are causing pain and suffering because they make you feel guilty, it is time to consider breaking free. Surely God values you and wants you to value yourself. If it is impossible to value who you are in the context of your religious community, it is time to find another place to express and nurture your spiritual self.

Ingrid's story illustrates how a religious community can be the source of debilitating toxic guilt.

Ingrid's Story

A pastor phoned me for consultation. He had been seeing a woman named Ingrid, who was new to his congregation, for spiritual counseling. Ingrid told the pastor that she had been a member of a fundamentalist Christian tradition all her life and was married to a man with the same background. Their religious community had standards of right and wrong that no longer made sense to her. Church members were judgmental, rigid, and self-righteous.

Ingrid had been miserable in her marriage for years, and now she was having an affair with a man at her workplace. She loved him, and he was in love with her; he begged her to leave her husband so they could have a life together. Ingrid longed to leave her husband, but she clung to the belief that divorce was wholly unacceptable to God and an unforgivable sin.

The pastor tried to help her see that there were other ways to look at her dilemma. He explained that divine love was compassionate and forgiving in nature, but Ingrid was unable to comprehend a religious perspective that differed from what she had been taught as a child. After months of agony, she decided she couldn't forsake her religious prohibition against divorce. In an attempt to right her wrong, she confessed the affair to her husband, who was still a faithful member of the church she had left. He rebuked her, telling her that she was a fallen woman and a sinner outside the love of God. "You got yourself into this mess," he growled. "Now you can get yourself out!"

Ingrid's new pastor was worried. His parishioner's mental health was dangerously deteriorating. She was so depressed that her thought processes were impaired. She wasn't taking care of herself, even neglecting personal hygiene, and she seldom left the house. Torn between her love for the other man and the absolute belief that God would punish her for that love, she was convinced she would never see heaven. (Suicide was not a threat because of her belief that she would go to hell if she killed herself.) What could the frustrated pastor do?

Analyzing Ingrid's Guilt

While Ingrid's story is a severe case, it illustrates how belief in an inflexible religious perspective can create toxic guilt. This unfortunate woman was stuck in spiritual agony, unable to move in a direction that would be life-affirming. Although she tried to escape the prohibitions of a faith she could no longer embrace, the guilt she felt for breaking the rules clung to her with tenacity. By the time she reached out for help, she was so emotionally drained and physically exhausted that she didn't have the strength to break free.

I wish I could relate a better ending to Ingrid's story, but the last time I spoke with the pastor he told me that Ingrid continued to languish alone at home, still married to a man she didn't love.

Sometimes I think I can hear God stomping her foot and shouting, "*No!* That's not what I meant!" in response to the teachings and tenets of some faith traditions. If you are trapped by guilt because of your faith tradition, your story does not have to have an unhappy ending. You can lay down the heavy burden you are carrying and escape. The five steps outlined in subsequent chapters will chart your course to freedom.

11

But They Won't Be Able to Function Without Me

People who want to move often don't because they feel too guilty. They worry about what the move would do to others: *How will the woman down the street get her prescriptions filled if I leave? How will my mother react to me being so far away?*

The same is often true for people who want to change jobs. They worry so much about how their decision will affect others that they are paralyzed. *The office would fall apart if I left! How could they possibly get on without me?*

It's hard to leave a job when the good opinion of others matters so much. *What would people think of me if I leave such a lucrative, stable job? Will they think I'm crazy, or selfish, or worse? How could I face my parents, wife, and kids if I quit? My income might go down and never recover. We might have to downsize—buy a smaller house, get rid of a car, change our whole lifestyle. How could I do that to them?*

Young adults may want to go away to college, or move out and get a job, but do neither because they don't want to upset their parents. Although moving away from home and hometown may be a healthy step toward independence and adulthood, it is particularly hard for some young adults because they feel responsible for their parents' well-being. And not all parents encourage healthy steps toward adulthood. Reacting to their own needs instead of the needs of their children, they subtly (or not so subtly) discourage a move away.

Married people with families may want to move away to pursue career opportunities or for other reasons but feel guilty about leaving their parents and extended families. Moreover, upsetting their children's routines can evoke enough guilt to be daunting. They imagine telling the kids and know what the scenario would be—tears and wailing about leaving friends and activities, possible threats of running away, accusations of them being the most selfish and horrible parents on the planet, and assurances that their children's lives are ruined forever.

Seniors may want to move away when they retire but feel guilty about leaving their children, who may have come to depend on them, or their aged parents, who need them now more than ever.

Maybe you have contemplated moving or changing jobs but have told yourself it just isn't practical or possible. Take the following quiz to see if there's a chance that guilt is behind your reluctance to take your dreams seriously.

Does Toxic Guilt Keep You Trapped in the Same Old Routine?

Answer the following questions to see if guilt might be keeping you from making a change you really want.

- Do you frequently fantasize about moving or changing jobs?
- Have you done any research about moving or changing jobs? (For example: gone online, sent off for brochures, visited places you'd like to move to, informally interviewed people in a job you'd relish, and so on.)
- Have you discussed your desire to move or change jobs with some people but not with important others because you

think they'd be upset? (For example: your spouse, parents, children, best friend, lover, and so on.)

- Does the fear of failure keep you from moving or changing jobs? (You constantly ask yourself: *what would people think of me if this didn't work out?*)
- Does the risk of upsetting others keep you from moving or changing jobs?
- Do you feel selfish when you contemplate moving or changing jobs?
- Do you worry about how others would see you if you moved or changed jobs? (You might think they'd call you uncaring, flighty, selfish, irresponsible, crazy, and so on.)
- Are you depressed because you want to move or change jobs but don't dare?
- Have you already moved or left your job emotionally, although in reality there is nothing in place for such a change?
- Do you feel energized, invigorated, and excited when you daydream about moving or changing jobs?
- Do you have a well-thought-out plan for moving or changing jobs but find you can't initiate even the first step?
- Is moving or changing jobs a real possibility, but you keep telling yourself it isn't?

If you answered yes to three or more questions, it is probable that guilt has you trapped in the same old routine.

People can get as locked into the wrong place or the wrong job as they can into the wrong marriage. Moving or leaving a job can evoke as much guilt as divorcing a spouse, if those who depend on you might suffer. Concern about the consequences for others or what they might think can keep people stuck in a place they don't want to be or married to jobs they hate.

A person's work is a large piece of his or her life. Our work defines us in many ways; it validates us as well. If that work is not satisfying and does not allow us to express who we are, it can be a giant siphon, draining the joy out of life.

A sense of place defines us as well. We want to live where the weather, political climate, topography, and social and religious culture suit us. Most people don't want to feel like a fish out of water—we want to fit in where we live. It can be equally important to live close to family or special friends, and a move may be required in order to do it. If we are trapped in the wrong place, no matter what the reason is, we suffer.

Implications for Moving or Changing Jobs

If guilt prevents you from moving or changing jobs, your life is diminished and important relationships may be at risk. Studies have shown that it is a negative sign for the future of a marriage if one partner prevents the other from realizing his or her dreams. Interestingly, it is worse if the husband prevents the wife from realizing her dreams. Although moving or changing jobs are not the only dreams a person might have, they are certainly not uncommon.

If you want to move or change jobs but are paralyzed by guilt, you will find a step-by-step process in Part III that can lead you to mobility. The following story illustrates the tangled mess that occurred when guilt interfered with Stephanie's husband's desire to move and get a new job.

Stephanie's Story

I coached twenty-five-year-old Stephanie through a difficult divorce. Her husband had left her for another woman. She'd had no idea the marriage was in jeopardy and was completely blind-sided. She was also devastated because she loved her husband.

One year after the divorce, she came back to see me to put clo-sure on the painful experience once and for all. Looking back over the landscape of her failed marriage, her vision was much clearer: she and her husband should have moved away.

Stephanie was an only child and very close to her parents. She and her husband, Kevin, moved into a house down the street from them right after they married. The young couple spent a lot of time with her parents—way too much time, as it turned out. Kevin and Stephanie did not develop couple friends their own age; instead, they did everything with her parents.

Kevin was offered a promotion with his company that required relocation. He was elated about the prospect of moving, and of moving up the ladder, but Stephanie balked. Although she never discussed with her parents the possibility of her and Kevin mov-ing away, she knew they would not be able to accept such an idea. Family rules and regulations don't always have to be articulated to be known.

Stephanie could not leave her parents, so reluctantly Kevin passed on the promotion. Now, a year after their divorce, Stepha-nie could see that was when things between them began to change. She wondered aloud what the outcome might have been if she had not allowed her guilt about leaving her parents to prevail.

Analyzing Stephanie's Guilt

Stephanie was caught in the middle. If she sided with her parents, her husband would be displeased, and if she sided with her hus-band, her parents would be hurt. In the end, guilt made the deci-sion for her. She would feel more guilty about leaving her parents than she would about disappointing her husband, since she felt she owed them loyalty for all they had done for her. Toxic guilt deceived her into believing she was doing the right thing, but she regretted it later.

Stephanie's situation is not uncommon. People get caught in the middle between parents and spouses all the time. It is crucial that you decide what your priority is and where your deepest loyalties lie.

Many people's dreams of retirement and the start of a new life go up in smoke when they experience guilt over leaving aged parents, adult children, or grandchildren. Fantasies of the future collide with what they think they owe others. The dilemma is intensified by the reality that time is slipping away, and the good health of youth right along with it. These seniors are trapped by guilt just when the possibility of freedom is right in front of them.

My Story

Two years after divorcing my first husband, I met my current husband. Thankfully, it is possible to find happiness the second time around. We are sad about all the years we didn't have together but grateful that we found each other.

Some people love the ocean and some love the mountains. Although we live in the Midwest, my husband is a mountain person who took me to Colorado shortly after we met. We've been going each year ever since, and I, too, fell in love with the mountains. My daughter moved to Colorado, and when she married and had a child, the pull of Colorado became even greater.

We began to dream of living there some day. At first it was a whimsical fantasy, but as the years went by we began to think we could make it happen. As retirement loomed closer and closer, we started looking for land to buy. After several years of serious searching we found the perfect spot, not far from my daughter's family and right in the area we love the most, with mountain views in three directions. Miraculously, it was for sale. But when we bought the property, the guilt set in.

I have struggled with guilt all my life. I worked long and hard to overcome my guilt-ridden nature and felt rather smug about my progress. But pride goes before a fall, and fall I did. I found myself trapped by guilt again, caught between my parents and my husband.

I'll explain: I was double-lucky in the parent department and have always had a close relationship with both of my wonderful parents. They live near us in the town where I grew up. My husband and I see them frequently and always enjoy their company. When we began thinking seriously about retiring in the mountains, I had a lot of soul-searching to do. I have deep roots in my hometown. My two siblings live here; I have friends from as far back as elementary school; I am the third generation of my family in our church; I have history here.

But most of all, I searched my soul about moving away from my parents. Octogenarians now, they needed me. How could I leave them? I vacillated for months and finally decided I could leave my hometown and community of dear friends, but not until my parents were gone. So that became the plan. However, time passed, my parents lived on, and my husband was retiring soon. Push was coming to shove. Caught between what I thought I owed my parents and what I thought I owed my husband, I agonized over my dilemma. I was trapped by guilt in every direction.

I finally escaped by following my own advice—thinking through the five steps and marshaling my support system. I also learned a helpful new technique, which I call the "Rule of Should," that I will share with you here.

The Rule of Should

I attended a weeklong conference on spirituality and psychology and came to know one of the presenters, Nancy Morrison, M.D.

We had a conversation one day, and I shared my dilemma with her. I told her I felt trapped because I thought I should move with my husband so that he could realize a lifelong dream of living in the mountains, but I also thought I should stay in my hometown to take care of my parents.

"Let's put a different twist on that," she said. "Instead of saying 'I should do this or that,' try saying, '*If* I should do this or that, *what would happen?*'"

With her frame of reference, my question became: *if I should* stay in my hometown until my parents are gone, what would happen? The answer was that my parents would continue to age and decline until they die, and that might take years. I would be available to care for them, but my husband and I would continue to long for the mountains. We would continue to age as well, and by the time my parents died, we might be too ill or old ourselves to make such a move. Therefore, our dream would be lost.

On the other hand, *if I should* move to the mountains with my husband, we would have the excitement of building a home together and the joy of living in a place we love. It would be an adventure to live someplace new. We would realize our dream, and I could visit my parents often.

My husband is retiring in a few months, and we are preparing to move. We are working on house plans and will break ground as soon as possible. I am not guilt-free about moving away from my aged parents, but my parents have other children here and I feel I am doing the right thing for my husband and me; that is very comforting.

The Rule of Should helped me make my decision and break free from guilt. If you are caught on the horns of a dilemma and wonder what to do, try using the Rule of Should. It will shed light on your situation.

The following story is an example of how guilt can keep people stuck in the wrong job.

Matt's Story

Matt was a pharmaceutical salesman for an international company. He was successful and well-compensated. His yearly bonus was well over most people's annual salary. His company provided everything—new cars, amazing health and dental insurance, and luxurious incentive vacations. He had it all, but he hated his job.

A job was not all Matt had. He also had a wife and two young children. His wife loved his job—and the lifestyle that went with it.

By the time Matt came to see me, he'd been harboring his secret for about two years. Nobody knew he found his work to be meaningless. No one knew his heart's desire.

Matt wanted to be a teacher. He dreamed of teaching troubled youth—high school, he thought. During college he had worked summers as an Outward Bound counselor, and he remembered the feeling of making a difference in somebody's life. He thought he would be good at it, but he was terrified of the thought of telling his wife. How could he disrupt her life? A teacher's salary would be a far cry from the income he currently earned. His friends and family would not support his desire to make a difference in the world; they'd think he'd lost his mind. Matt was dismally unhappy.

Analyzing Matt's Guilt

Matt was caught between living his dream and living out the role he thought he had to play for his family. Although his desire to become a teacher was a noble one, it would mean a significant lifestyle change for his family. Matt was sure his wife would be horrified if she knew, so his dream became a dark secret. But since work has such a prominent place in defining who we are, Matt risked losing part of his authentic identity by remaining in a job that he hated and that was meaningless to him. Psychologically, the risk was huge.

I encouraged Matt to confront his guilt and share his dream with his wife. I assured him that he had as much right to his dream as his wife had to her lifestyle. I told him I thought he was probably correct in his assessment of his wife's reaction and the reaction of his friends and family, but I predicted he could manage the fallout. I also predicted that he could let go of other people's disapproval in order to do what he needed to do. And I taught him how to protect himself from toxic guilt in the future.

Matt followed the steps of escaping toxic guilt and walked out of a job that was toxic to his spirit. He downsized and bought a smaller house. Once he combined the proceeds from the sale of his house with his savings, he had enough money to go back to school for his teaching degree without having to work. His wife adjusted to the change in their lifestyle and eventually was able to enthusiastically support her husband in his new venture. I love happy endings!

If you feel your dreams of the future are slipping away, take heart: it is not too late. Climbing the five steps in Part III will give you legs to stand on.

12

So, Whose House Are You Going to This Thanksgiving?

Almost everyone knows this one. It's the guilt you feel when you contemplate not going to Mom's, or Dad's, or Grandma's . . . for Christmas, or birthdays, or Sunday night dinner. The rationale for holiday plans is often revealed in conversations like the following.

Spouse to spouse: "We were at your mom's for four days last Thanksgiving. Why are we only staying two days at my mom's this year?"

Divorced father to adult child: "You were at your mom's the last two Christmases in a row. Don't you think you could manage to spend this Christmas with me?"

Statements like these can make a puppet out of a business executive or turn a mild-mannered homemaker into a freaked-out caricature of herself. Sometimes the traditional where-are-we-going-for-Christmas fight comes out of the attic as reliably as the tree lights and bulbs. Conversations about a holiday or a summer vacation can instigate all-out war in the most copacetic couple when in-laws are keeping score.

Many people find their way to the therapist's office over these tit-for-tat forced marches. I do not see this situation getting better in the future—young couples really have it tough these days. People live longer than ever before, so a young family may need to split their time not only between parents and grandparents, but with great-grandparents as well. With the divorce rate still at about 50 percent, couples may share their time with as many as ten households!

When You Want to End Holiday Disagreements and Disasters

Here is a brief quiz to find out if you are trapped in the throes of "the most wonderful time of the year":

- Do you dread holidays because of the predictable conflict with your spouse or partner about who goes where when?
- Does the need to please your in-laws dictate your holiday schedule?
- Does the need to please your parents dictate your holiday schedule?
- Does the need to please your children dictate your holiday schedule?
- Does the need to please your spouse dictate your holiday schedule?
- Does the need to make everyone happy at holidays rob you of being happy?
- Do you want to start your own holiday traditions but feel you can't?
- Do you often get sick (for example: migraines, stomach flu, depression, colds) during the holidays?
- Does the need to include problematic family members at holiday events cause stress and family discord?
- When holiday season approaches, do you often say to yourself, *It's just not worth it!*—but you can't (or won't) do anything to make it different?

- At the holidays, do you feel trapped by family traditions that you would love to escape?
- Do you fight with your spouse every Christmas, Thanksgiving, Kwanzaa, or Hanukkah about where and how you will celebrate the holiday?
- Would you love to just stay home for the holidays but feel you can't?

If you answered yes to three or more questions, it is probable that guilt is robbing you of celebrating the holidays as you would like.

Most of us place a very high value on holidays and how they are spent. We fantasize about how the holidays should look and feel— and we have plenty of models for the ideal in literature, movies, songs, and TV stories. When our holiday expectations fall short of how we think things should be, we are disillusioned and feel somehow inadequate. Feelings of disappointment run particularly high if holiday events are out of our control.

Why would anyone allow their holiday schedule to be directed by someone else? Guilt is the answer.

Taking Charge of Family Visits and Events

The need to please extended family, parents, grandparents, in-laws, children, and friends can turn your holiday time into anything but what you want. There's truth to the lyrics in the late Rick Nelson's classic song "Garden Party": "You see, ya can't please everyone, so you got to please yourself." Maybe that should be the motto for people plagued with toxic guilt, especially when it comes to celebrating holidays. When you learn to "please yourself" at the holidays you will not only experience a sense of liberation, but you may also be able to enjoy your extended family much more because you will not resent them as much.

Many people lose the holiday spirit as they take on the impossible task of pleasing everyone. Family visits at times other than holidays can be plagued with similar problems, too. See if you find an all-too-familiar scenario in the following story.

Ryan and Monica's Story

Ryan's parents lived in Kansas City, Missouri, and Monica's lived in Little Rock, Arkansas. Ryan and Monica and their two small children lived in Springfield, Missouri, midway between their parents. The couple came to see me about conflict over family visits.

Ryan's parents were good, hardworking people. They were not connected to extended family, and what social life they had, including holiday celebrations, centered on their church. They had Thanksgiving dinner in the church fellowship hall, and on Christmas Eve they attended the choral recital. There is not a thing wrong with this, but to Ryan and Monica it was right up there with having a root canal—they dreaded the experience.

Monica's parents were very close to extended family and had a wide circle of friends. Active members of their country club, they played golf, entertained frequently, and enjoyed dining out. Ryan and Monica had a great time visiting her parents. There were always people in and out of the house and lots of laughter, fun, and frolic. Monica's parents usually had friends or family in for dinners or backyard barbecues when Ryan and Monica visited.

The holidays were especially enjoyable. On Halloween they went all-out with a costume party, complete with prizes for the best costumes. It was a celebration that Ryan and Monica seldom missed. At Thanksgiving the table groaned with food and guests.

Visits to Ryan's parents were a dismal contrast. Typically, Ryan would go on long runs out of sheer boredom, leaving Monica and the children at home with his mother. Since her mother-in-law was fairly obsessive about her house (even Ryan admitted it looked like it had never been lived in), Monica had to watch the kids' every move, forever admonishing them to "be careful" and "don't touch." By the end of the visit, the kids were fussy, Ryan was frustrated, and Monica was exhausted.

The problem was that Ryan's mother kept score about the frequency of visits to Monica's parents and the time spent with them. If she discerned that there was even a day's discrepancy between time spent at her house and time at Monica's parents, she'd call Ryan and all hell would break loose. She didn't rant or rave or threaten; it was worse than that. She'd put Ryan on a major guilt trip by accusing him of not loving his own parents as much as he loved his wife's. Guilt-ridden and angry, Ryan would blame Monica and a major conflict would ensue. It had become a pattern. Clearly, the couple was caught in the trap of guilt and pleasing others.

Analyzing Ryan's Guilt

Ryan felt so guilty about preferring to spend more time with Monica's parents that he allowed his mother to dictate the "rules" of family visits. Attempting to relieve his guilty conscience, he gave his mother a tremendous amount of power.

When pleasing or appeasing parents takes precedence over pleasing or appeasing a spouse, something is out of kilter. Although it is preferable if both partners in a marriage honor their in-laws and support their spouse's relationship with his or her parents, the feelings of the parents should not be the most important consideration.

A principal rule in a marriage relationship is that each partner should be the top priority to the other. A husband should know he comes first with his wife, and a wife should be assured she comes first with her husband. There will be times when it makes sense to bow to the wishes of parents or others, but the prevailing climate should be that the spouse's wishes take precedence.

I see plenty of marital conflict that revolves around this issue: *He won't stand up to his mother for me!* or *Every time her dad says "Jump" she says "How high?"* Many people feel that disappointing or displeasing a parent is more difficult than upsetting a spouse. It's all about guilt, and it's all wrong.

Ryan was so bored at his parents' house that he escaped the best way he could and left his wife to deal with his mother. No wonder Monica was resentful! In order to put things right with his wife, Ryan had to stop being a passenger on his mother's guilt trips.

In Chapter 16 on claiming territory, you'll see how Ryan and Monica devised a plan that put them in charge of how they spent the holidays. If you are exhausted with attempts to please everyone, learn how to take control of your life around the holidays and still be respectful to extended family. Ryan and Monica's plan may work wonders for you!

13

But It'll Kill Them to Find Out I'm Gay

Guilt and fear traps many gays and lesbians in a life of denial for far too long. Feeling guilty about their same-gender attractions and fearful of the harsh response of the prevailing culture, it is no wonder that many young gays and lesbians don't initially want to claim their sexual identity. Sadly, it's often only after a torturous journey through the long, dark valley of denial and self-castigation that gays and lesbians can finally be themselves.

The self-concept of many gay youth is challenged because they believe that their same-sex orientation somehow makes them bad or wrong or immoral. Some are so overwhelmed by a negative self-image that they deny their desires and force themselves into heterosexual relationships. The end result is pain and suffering for everyone involved. Others do much worse: suicide rates are higher among gay youth than in the general population.

When You Want to Claim Your Sexual Identity

Human beings are sexual beings; it is a big part of who we are. If you are gay or lesbian, acknowledging your sexual identity is a crucial step in your personal growth and development. First, you must free yourself from guilt. Then you can begin to build a personal strategy for coming out if that is what you want. I'll help you with the guilt piece and give you some ideas for revealing who you really are.

Is Guilt About Your Sexual Identity Causing Problems in Your Life?

Answer the following questions to see if guilt over claiming your sexual identity may be limiting your ability to live a satisfying life.

- Do you long to tell someone important in your life (such as your parents, a friend, a sibling, or a colleague) that you are gay?
- Are you sick and tired of pretending to be heterosexual?
- Have you chastised yourself for being attracted to those of the same gender?
- Have you had heterosexual relationships in an effort to "make yourself straight"?
- Have you been attracted to the same gender for as long as you can remember?
- When you watch a love scene in a movie, are you attracted to the character who's the same gender as you?
- Have you tried to squelch your same-sex attraction in every way you know how, to no avail?
- Do openly gay or lesbian individuals or couples make you envious?
- Have you visited a place where homosexuality is acceptable, just to see what it felt like to be in an atmosphere of toler-

ance? (For example: a bar or club; a party or social gathering; a religious community; a town, city, or country; and so on.)

- Have you had a sexual relationship with a same-sex partner?
- Are you drawn to books and movies about same-sex relationships?
- Do you fantasize about being out?
- Are you irresistibly drawn to members of the same sex?
- Do you often think that your life is a lie?
- Do you fantasize about same-sex relationships?
- Do you think God is displeased with you or will punish you because of your same-sex attractions?
- Do you wish you lived someplace where homosexuality was more acceptable?
- Are you in a heterosexual marriage but know you're gay or lesbian?

If you answered yes to five or more questions, it is likely that you are gay or lesbian and feel guilty about claiming your sexuality.

As you can see, some questions in the quiz are aimed at people who aren't sure whether they're gay, and some questions are for those who do know but keep it a secret out of guilt. The quiz is structured that way because the guilt of same-sex attraction can obscure the truth and cause people to doubt what they think or feel. Remember, two of the characteristics of toxic guilt are that it "twists the truth and blinds us to the reality of the situation" and "makes us doubt ourselves" (Chapter 1). Many people who find themselves irresistibly drawn to members of the same sex feel so guilty about it that they become experts at hiding it from themselves. I have worked with a number of people who sought my counsel because they didn't know whether or not they were gay. In every case, the guilt of acknowledging their homosexuality was so great that it took therapy to help them break through it.

It is important to say that in the case of acknowledging homosexuality, guilt is not the only culprit. Shame can also be operative. Guilt is feeling wrong or bad about what we do or do not do, and shame is feeling wrong or bad about *who we are*. Since sexuality is an integral part of our identity, people who have same-sex attraction often feel bad or wrong about who they are as human beings. When toxic guilt and shame are both active, it is an all-out attack on a person's positive sense of self.

Claiming Your Sexual Identity

Escaping toxic guilt and claiming sexual identity is the only road to a satisfying and meaningful life for the majority of people who are gay or lesbian. People who deny their true sexual identity can never live authentically. They become perpetual imposters, lying to themselves and others about who they really are.

Thankfully, homosexuality is becoming more and more acceptable. Social and cultural norms continue to change for the better as more and more gay people claim their sexual identity and come out. But societal change comes slowly, and homosexuals still suffer from discrimination and prejudice.

Todd's story is typical of the pain and suffering that can occur when toxic guilt keeps someone from living in their true sexual identity.

Todd's Story

Todd was a senior in college when he came to me for therapy. His father was the high school football coach in their small hometown. Todd, an only child, was very close to his tight-knit family. Thin and delicate, Todd didn't exactly live up to the athletic aspirations his father had for him. His father was determined to make Todd into an athlete. Hopelessly optimistic, the father pressured his son year after year.

When I first saw Todd he was a wreck. His slender face, big green eyes, and anxious stare made him look like a frightened kitten. He explained that he was in a committed relationship with Scott and had been for over a year. His parents did not know. Having failed as the macho athlete his father hoped for, how could he possibly tell his father he was gay?

Scott took Todd's reluctance to come out to his parents as a personal affront. For Scott, it was a sign that he didn't really mean that much to Todd. Meanwhile, Todd was so anxious that he couldn't concentrate, couldn't eat, and wasn't sleeping well either. Caught between a rock and a hard place, Todd couldn't see a way out. How could he reassure his partner without risking almost certain rejection from his father?

Analyzing Todd's Guilt

Todd felt guilty on two counts: he knew he would disappoint his father if he came out to him, and he knew he would disappoint Scott if he did not. As I walked with him through the five steps, he sorted out his feelings. He had been a disappointment to his father all his life for not being the kind of male his father valued most, a jock. Although Todd tried again and again to live up to his father's expectations, he never could. In many ways, his father did not know his son at all.

Scott, on the other hand, knew exactly who Todd was and valued and respected him greatly. In his relationship with Scott, Todd felt seen and heard by an important male figure for the first time in his life. He was not willing to lose that.

With support from Scott and other friends, Todd went home one weekend and came out to his father. His father's reaction was just as he predicted: denial, anger, and finally tears. His father told his mother, and their solution was to insist that Todd go to therapy to get "fixed." When Todd confessed he was already in therapy and had been for some time, they were baffled.

Their next ploy was to invite their pastor and a few members of the congregation over for an "intervention"—God and the church would "fix" him. (Todd was prepared for these tactics, which he anticipated when we worked through Step Three, "Brace for the Storm.") Todd stood his ground (which he learned to do in Step Two, "Claim Territory"), and the church committee left, exasperated.

Finally, and sadly, Todd's parents told him to leave and not come back until he had changed; they also cut off his funding for college.

Todd was sad and upset about their response but reported that he also felt a great sense of relief and felt "clean inside." He got a job and applied for financial aid. Before he graduated, Todd and his parents reconciled. Although the topic of his sexual identity is taboo between Todd and his parents, they were willing to meet Scott and even allowed him to visit in their home.

I applaud the courage of gay and lesbian people who are determined to be who they are in the world. I hope the information presented here will lend support, encouragement, and a plan of escape to those who are still trapped by toxic guilt.

14

But They'll Be So Ashamed of Me

The guilt that accompanies the difficult decision of what to do about an unplanned pregnancy can destroy a woman's emotional health. The social, cultural, political, and religious pressure on a woman with an unplanned pregnancy can be so intense that she can't make a good decision for herself. Every option is fraught with guilt-inducing consequences. If she decides to terminate the pregnancy she must face the condemnation of those who would condemn her as a "baby-killer." If she decides to keep the baby and is not married, she bears the humiliation of being an "unwed mother" and possibly all of the parenting responsibilities. If she decides to keep the baby and is married, her life will probably change. She may have to go back to work, quit work, or make other significant concessions. If she gives her baby up for adoption, she may be tagged with labels like "selfish," "shallow," "irresponsible," or worse.

When a woman has decided that termination is the best option, the cultural and religious taboos can be overwhelming. There are religious communities that are as loving and forgiving as a pit of vipers. They claim to know the Truth not only for themselves but for everyone else. They are all too happy to make the decisions for a woman with an unwanted pregnancy. Women who make different choices (and those who help them) are reviled, cast into darkness and disgrace. Sometimes, they even get killed.

Women who decide to complete their pregnancy may be hypervigilant throughout it and blame themselves if the slightest thing goes wrong. If there's even the tiniest problem, they tell themselves they must have done this on purpose because they didn't really want this baby. The same is true for women who keep their babies: *it's my fault my baby is sick (or developmentally slow, or fussy); after all, I didn't want him in the first place.* If women give their babies up for adoption, the guilt is there as well: *how could I be a good person and give my baby away?*

Dealing with an Unplanned Pregnancy

Answer the following questions to see whether guilt might be keeping you from doing what you want to do with an unplanned pregnancy:

- Do you want to terminate your pregnancy but feel you can't?
- Do you think God will be displeased or punish you if you terminate your pregnancy?
- Does fear of upsetting your parents, lover, or others (such as members of your faith community and your pastor or priest) keep you from doing what you want to do about your unplanned pregnancy?
- Have you decided to keep your baby, but you second-guess yourself at the slightest provocation? (For example, you don't feel well and wonder if you did something on purpose to put yourself at risk for illness, or you forget to take your prenatal vitamins and chastise yourself for doing it intentionally.)
- Would you like to keep your baby, but you don't dare?
- Are important people in your life dismayed about your pregnancy and you are not, but you don't say anything?

- Do you want to give your baby up for adoption but haven't filled out the paperwork because you think everyone (God, your parents, faith community, friends, lover, and so on) will say you are a bad person or bad mother if you go through with it?
- Do you want to do one thing but your parents, spouse, lover, or others are pressuring you to do another, and you are stuck in the middle, unable to make a decision?
- Does the need to please others take precedence over *your* wishes and desires?
- Would you like to give your baby up for adoption, but you don't dare?
- Are important people in your life thrilled about your pregnancy when you are not, but you don't say anything?

If you answered yes to two or more questions, guilt may be clouding your decision about an unwanted pregnancy.

Criticism and fear of rejection from important others—parents and extended family, spouses, lovers, friends, acquaintances, and religious community members—keep some women with an unwanted pregnancy at the crossroads of despair. How do they dare to do what they want to do?

Remember from Chapter 4 that the need to think of ourselves as "good" and have others see us as "good" is powerful. People with toxic guilt are especially invested in being "good." And women in particular want to be seen as "good" women.

Some factions of the religious and political culture are all too happy to define what being a "good" woman is. Billboards, magazine ads, commercial spots on TV, books, and bumper stickers tell women how to think and feel about themselves in relation to an unwanted pregnancy:

- Abortion kills.
- It's a child, not a choice.

- What is "pro-family" about killing children?
- Choosy mothers choose life.
- Choose life, your mom did!

The message is clear: you are bad if you don't have your baby, no matter what. It is no wonder so many women are crushed by guilt under the weight of such shaming messages. Instead of thoughtfully considering all the options and all the possible consequences, some women turn a blind eye to their choices in order to avoid feeling guilty, and rush into a decision they regret later. This holds as true for women who decide to keep their baby without careful consideration as it does for those who get a "knee-jerk" abortion.

Breaking Free

It may take a village to raise a child, but it shouldn't take a village to decide what a woman should do with an unwanted pregnancy. It is a personal, private decision that belongs to the woman alone. (Although the decision should be hers alone, she will hopefully not be alone as she makes the decision. A woman with an unplanned pregnancy needs all the support she can get, no matter what she decides to do.)

I've had clients who wanted and needed to terminate a pregnancy rendered immobile by guilt, unable to take action. I've also had those who terminated a pregnancy long ago and have been besieged by guilt ever since. I've had a few who, against the advice and wishes of family and friends, decided to complete an unplanned pregnancy and either keep their baby or give it up for adoption. Each decision impacted the life of the woman forever. The conscience of the woman should dictate such an important decision—and not the guilty conscience!

The following story illustrates how guilt can isolate a woman with an unplanned pregnancy and leave her alone with one of the most important decisions in life.

Caroline's Story

Caroline, age twenty-three, and her boyfriend, Michael, had no intention of getting pregnant. She was diligent about taking the pill but somehow got pregnant anyway. Both were new college graduates in their first jobs. They had only been together about ten months and weren't even sure what their relationship meant at this point.

Caroline felt all alone. Although she was close to her mother, this was the one thing she could not share with her; she already knew how her mother felt about abortion. Making things worse, Caroline was Roman Catholic and had gone to parochial schools all her life. Although she did not agree with the church's stand on abortion, years of classes, sermons, and conversations had made an indelible impact.

Recently, she had seen a bumper sticker that was particularly disturbing. It said, "You can't be both Catholic and pro-choice." She loved her church and attended services regularly. If she terminated her pregnancy, she would have to keep it a closely guarded secret from her priest and everyone else. How could she continue to kneel in prayer at a church that condemned her? The guilt would be horrible.

Caroline thought she knew what she wanted to do—but she was frightened, guilt-ridden, and anguished. She had no impartial place to go with her questions. At such a crucial point in her life, this young woman had no one to turn to except her boyfriend and me, a stranger.

Analyzing Caroline's Guilt

Caroline both needed and deserved the freedom to make such an important decision without the burden of toxic guilt. It is a sad commentary that she could not count on the very people who mattered most in her life—her mother and her religious community—to stand by her as bastions of support while she wrestled with her options. I helped her examine her options and facilitated a discussion about the consequences of each.

Marriage was not an acceptable option. She loved Michael, but their relationship was new and she did not want it to be forced by an unplanned pregnancy. If the relationship did not work out, she would wind up being a single mother—she wasn't ready for that. She had dreams of a career in fashion design, and her new job as a buyer in a trendy boutique could launch her in the right direction. Frequent travel is the order of the day in the fashion industry; how could she devote the time needed to become successful in her career and be a good mother as well? She did not think she could. The thought of having a baby and giving it to someone else seemed so ludicrous to her that she took that option off the table right away. Although abortion seemed the best choice to her, the guilt was overwhelming.

I introduced her to the five steps of overcoming toxic guilt, and she worked through each one thoughtfully. Finally, with determination to chart the course of her life on her own terms, and with her boyfriend by her side for support, she terminated the pregnancy.

These eight guilt-inducing situations cause much suffering and anguish. If you are trapped in one or more of these situations, take heart. The following chapters will give you a plan of action and the tools you'll need to make a successful escape.

Part III

The Escape Plan

15

Step One:
Speak the Truth

The first step out of the guilt trap is to acknowledge exactly what's going on. Stop hiding the truth from yourself because you think the way you really feel makes you a bad person. When you have been honest with yourself, share your truth with someone you trust and respect; it may be a pastor, rabbi, therapist, mentor, family member, or friend.

Be gut-level honest and don't sugarcoat it: I'm miserable in my marriage. My kids are running my life and I can't stand it anymore. I hate college. I'm gay. I don't love my spouse anymore. This job is killing me and I want to quit. My friend is making me crazy. I'm in love with another man. I'm sick of my children. I'm having an affair. I'm pregnant.

Confession: An Overview

Contrary to what some people may think, confession is a wonderful concept. The emotional and spiritual benefits are truly life-affirming. While confession is at the heart of psychotherapy, psychology did not give birth to the idea—religion did. I'll discuss confession first as a religious practice and then explore the use of confession in psychotherapy.

Confession as a Religious Practice

References to confession are found throughout the Bible. Both the Old Testament and the New Testament admonish followers to confess the truth of their situation and the error of their ways. A restored relationship with God is promised, and a restored relationship with others is possible. The following quotes are from the New Revised Standard Version of the Bible and illustrate the importance of confession.

I confess my iniquity; I am sorry for my sin.

—*Psalms 38:18*

If we confess our sins, he who is faithful and just will forgive us our sins and cleanse us from all unrighteousness.

—*1 John 1:8*

Therefore confess your sins to one another, and pray for one another, so that you may be healed.

—*James 5:16*

The early Christian church thought confession was so important that it was institutionalized as a sacrament during the medieval period. Confession, also called penance, was seen as the remedy for the ills of the soul.

In the sacrament of penance, the penitent seeks the ear of a priest, who listens, forgives, and assigns reparations. It is important to note that the priest is a flesh-and-blood representative of *God's presence.* Many people have the mistaken notion that the priest takes on the role of God, which is not the case.

The Roman Catholic, Greek Orthodox, American Lutheran, and Episcopal/Anglican traditions offer sacramental confession. In the other Protestant churches, repentance and confession is personal, between the person and God alone. Although the confession of a remorseful heart to God alone is a valid approach, it omits the perhaps more difficult, but potentially more powerful, task of acknowledging the error of your ways to another of the flesh-and-bone variety who has been given authority by the community of believers to grant absolution.

It can be an anxiety-provoking proposition to make private confession to a priest, but many say it is worth it. The priest's absolution is reassurance of God's forgiveness.

Corporate or group confession is an integral part of worship in several faith traditions. Here is the lovely communal "Confession of Sin" from *The Book of Common Prayer* (Episcopal tradition). With this method, the congregation acknowledges their shortcomings aloud.

> Most merciful god, we confess that we have sinned against you in thought, word, and deed, by what we have done, and by what we have left undone. We have not loved you with our whole heart; we have not loved our neighbors as ourselves. We are truly sorry and we humbly repent. For the sake of your Son Jesus Christ, have mercy on us and forgive us; that we may delight in your will, and walk in your ways, to the glory of your Name. Amen.

For the religious person, an awareness of God's approval is crucial to a positive self-concept. When someone believes God is disappointed or angry, guilt prevails—and with it comes a sense of wrongness or badness about oneself. Confession, with its promise of forgiveness, restores a good relationship not only with God but also with oneself.

Confession and forgiveness go hand-in-hand because it is impossible to experience forgiveness without acknowledging the truth. In the confession/forgiveness process, the person confessing experiences the joy-filled quality of being pardoned and feels lighter, freer, more whole, and more loved. In general, life is back on the positive track.

Confession as a Psychological Practice

Psychology has long recognized the power of catharsis—the freeing of emotions that have been hidden, denied, or pushed away. Emotions held inside—especially strong negative emotions—can wreck havoc on the human psyche. Guilt, depression, anxiety, and physical ailments can be the consequence of unexpressed emotion.

When one confesses, one acknowledges or admits something that has been held inside. The revelation of that material to an accepting other is usually accompanied by an emotional release and a sense of liberation.

Therapists become confessors to their clients; certainly I have filled that position. In doing so, I have been humbled and moved by the transformation that often occurs in my clients when they bare their souls, and I do not judge them. As a person of faith and a therapist, when I feel it is appropriate I remind my clients that God is loving and forgiving.

Donna's Story

My new client spun on her heel and flopped down on the sofa with a helpless thud. "You've got to help me," she wailed. "I hate my kids!"

That was a quick confession, I thought to myself. *It must have been building up.*

Donna was a third-grade teacher with her own third-grader and a four-year-old at home.

"Katy purposefully acts out in public. Yesterday she tore up and down the aisles at the grocery store like a banshee! I wouldn't buy candy for Jenny at the checkout, and she sat in the cart and screamed. I can't take it anymore!" She dissolved into tears.

I handed her a tissue. "Of course you hate your kids," I said, laughing. "Everybody does."

She looked up, mascara running in little brown-tinged rivers down her face. Dabbing, she said, "Really?"

"Sure," I responded. "Goes with the territory."

She exhaled like air escaping from a beach ball; I could see the tension disappear. Then the floodgates opened and the angst poured out: She felt guilty that she loved her job; she should want to be a stay-at-home mom. She felt guilty that the little one was in day care all day and the older one was in an after-school program strangers had her kids more than she did. She felt guilty that they misbehaved so much; surely if she were a better mother, they wouldn't. She felt guilty that she didn't like them much these days; that was against the "good-mother rules." She felt guilty that so much of her energy went to the children in her classroom; it should be going to her own. She felt guilty that she was exhausted and irritable at the end of the day; she should be more patient. She felt guilty that when she did discipline them, she often exploded; she knew better than that. The poor woman was besieged by guilt.

By the end of the session, tiny signs of improvement were apparent. It wasn't because I did something miraculous—it was because she confessed to what she thought was a litany of sins. When I accepted her confession in a supportive, nonjudgmental way, she felt validated. When I assured her that most parents at one time or another don't like their kids one bit, her face lit up like a slot machine.

I could have been her mother, her pastor, a best friend, or anyone she trusted. But Donna's crimes and misdemeanors were, in her mind, so heinous that she couldn't risk telling anyone but a mental health professional who was outside her circle of friends and relatives.

In the sessions that followed, we worked through the rest of the five steps, and now Donna has a grip on her guilt. Her guilt no longer keeps her from disciplining her children in a reasonable, healthy way, and it doesn't dictate the way she feels about herself.

Journaling: A Truth-Telling Tool

If the thought of telling someone the truth about your situation and feelings is so intimidating that you know you won't do it, there is a way to ease into the process. If you express your feelings in writing first, verbalizing them to another will probably come much more easily once you feel ready.

Journaling is not the same as keeping a diary. Diaries are written accounts of daily life, while journaling is a written account of emotional life. Often, keeping a diary comes with the unpleasant pressure to make daily entries. There is no schedule required in journaling; one only makes entries when there are emotions that need to be expressed. For some people it may be a daily practice; for others days, weeks, or months may elapse between entries.

Journaling is effective for three reasons: First, it is cathartic because it allows expression and release of thoughts and feelings that are uncomfortable. Second, it helps the writer make sense out of the thoughts and feelings that tend to float in and out of consciousness. In the process of writing, those thoughts and feelings must be organized into logical syntax, which clarifies their meaning. The writer gains an understanding of his or her own emotions. Third, journaling can help the writer prepare for verbal confession to another person.

Many people report that they feel more comfortable with the material after it is committed to the written word. Reviewing the entries several times can also be helpful.

If you would like to try journaling, I suggest that you choose your journal carefully. Some people use the lovely cloth-covered blank journals usually found in bookstores or specialty shops. Others are more comfortable with simple spiral-bound notebooks. Still others prefer to journal on their computers.

Journaling is a private affair. Be sure you are able to put your journal somewhere safe where unwelcome readers would not be apt to find it. Write in your journal whenever you find yourself mulling over situations and feelings that are painful, distressing, or unclear.

Many people find that when it is time to confess the truth of their situation to another, it is easier to read aloud from their journal than it is to express the material in unstructured conversation. If you decide to confess to another by reading what you have written in your journal, I encourage you to read your entries out loud rather than inviting the other person to read your material. When you are the reader, it increases your participation in the experience and helps you own the material.

Housekeeping

Do you really want your guilt trip to end? Then confession is not an option—it is a requirement. If you are Roman Catholic, Greek Orthodox, Lutheran, Episcopal, or Anglican, the sacrament of confession may be your best option. If you are not, or do not choose to participate in sacramental confession, you might want to schedule a session with a therapist or lunch with a trusted friend. You might consider ritualizing these meetings so that you meet with your "confessor" several times a year.

I clean my interior house every week on Sunday mornings when I pray the general confession at church. But that's not enough for me. I also have spiritual directors who help me with deep cleaning when I need to take the time to get into every nook and cranny and do a really thorough, really comprehensive job of it.

Spiritual direction is a wonderful enrichment to the life of faith, and it's widely available. In the Christian tradition it was an ancient custom that reached a peak of popularity in the Middle Ages and then faded away. It's been enjoying a revival of interest and practice in the past few years. The idea is to select a person who is farther down the spiritual path than you are and establish a regular time to meet with them. Spiritual directors are holy listeners who accompany their charges as they travel the road of faith.

My spiritual directors are a retired priest and his wife. I meet with them every month for an hour to talk about whatever is on my mind and inevitably confess a thing or two. I tell them about my nasty attitude, or maybe relate a dark thought or ten. I ask questions and seek advice; often we launch into a lively conversation about a spiritual issue. At the end of the hour, we join hands and pray. I leave feeling refreshed every time. Not only do I have spiritual directors, but I am also a spiritual director myself and have people who come and meet with me. In fact, my spiritual directors have their own spiritual directors. It becomes a rather lovely network.

There are many other options for confession. A group of like-minded, supportive friends can be an invaluable resource. Traditional women's groups like sewing or craft circles, exercise groups, bridge or mah-jongg clubs, and book clubs can serve this function very well. Men can make use of hunting trips, fishing outings, poker games, and men's groups in their church.

These groups require no leader, demand no homework, and are already part and parcel of a social support network. The specific format isn't important; what is important is that it's a group of friends, which is often a safe and supportive atmosphere in which to confess.

As you would imagine, it takes a group some time to develop an atmosphere of intimacy and trust. That's natural. It is not wise to join a group and immediately begin to bare your soul. All close relationships take time and effort, but belonging to a group of friends you trust and enjoy is well worth the effort.

A practice of confession can also occur one-on-one, between friends. Maggie is a dear friend with whom I practice confession on a regular basis. We meet once a month for lunch without fail. Our lunches are wonderful refueling opportunities; we share our lives and confess the angst that accompanies the good stuff. I leave those encounters feeling that my batteries have been recharged.

Twice a year Maggie and I go on retreat. We prefer predominantly silent retreats, so we visit either a nearby monastery, one of several retreat houses in the area, or a nice resort. Our pattern is to maintain silence except at meals, when we come together for conversation and yes, confession. It's at those times that we really get down to the depths of our souls and dig out the sludge that collects on the bottom. Maggie says she "cleans all her cupboards" on our retreats; so do I. Other friends might want to go on a cruise, a trip to the beach, or a wilderness trek. A change of scene can provide the freedom to confess.

You'll notice that confession is a lot of work. It requires intentionality and practice. It is high-risk behavior. But for folks navigating their way out of a guilt trip, it is essential as a compass in the wilderness.

James's Story

"You'll find I don't talk much." James, my new client, squirmed nervously on the sofa, crossing and uncrossing his legs. "My wife tells me I don't talk to her. . . . Well, what's the point? She never listens anyway."

"So you don't feel heard?"

"No, never. . . . I feel so guilty to be here, to talk about this. It will sound like I don't like her—my wife. That's not true! She's a good person, she's a good mother. I care for her deeply . . . but I can't take it anymore!"

"Sounds like you have a lot to say," I ventured.

For the next forty-five minutes the poor guy didn't draw a breath. His tale poured out like sand through a sieve. His wife was moody;

he couldn't predict from one day to the next what kind of mood she'd be in when she woke up. If she was in one of her bad moods, the whole household suffered.

She was extremely sensitive and felt slighted or disrespected with the least provocation. Things that most people ignore or let go wounded her to the core. Although she could not take even a hint of criticism, she dished it out without mercy. When she and James got into an argument, she went for the jugular and said horrible and demeaning things about him.

She was also inclined to go overboard when she was angry with the children and say mean things that a parent shouldn't say to a child. James and the kids walked on eggshells to keep from upsetting her or making her mad. He tried to be the buffer between her and the children and was forever trying to smooth the water and keep the peace. She was jealous of the good relationship he had with his children, especially his daughter, and invented ways to sabotage it. There was more, but James couldn't get the whole story told in one session.

The next session was similar. He related incident after incident about how his wife had made his life difficult, from the breakfast table to the bedroom.

James was a private man; I was the first person to hear his story. As the inventory of painful memories poured out, the guilt-induced apologies (like "I shouldn't be saying this," "She's really a good person," and "It's probably not her fault") decreased. I could see him relax as the tale unfolded. He stopped crossing his legs and shifting around, his eye contact with me improved, and the flush on his face and neck evaporated. He began to laugh a little.

Of course I only had James's side of the story about the relationship, but at least it was a beginning. My hope was that marital therapy would follow eventually. In confessing his dissatisfaction with the marriage, James had taken the first step out of the guilt trap. Now he was ready to formulate a plan of action—Step Two.

16

Step Two:
Claim Territory

This is the longest chapter in the book, and for a good reason: it is the most important. Learning to claim your emotional territory is like learning to ride a bike. First, you see others do it and wish you could do it too. Next, you examine the concept. If you are going to ride a bike you must understand how the wheels, pedals, and brakes work, and why. If you are claiming your emotional territory you must learn to stand up for yourself, make your own decisions, and do what you want to do. Then you find someone to help you get your balance and you practice, practice, practice. Finally, you're off on your own, feeling competent, confident, free, and joyful.

In Chapter 4, I discussed the importance of personal boundaries or emotional fences. I also said that people of the guilt-ridden variety don't have great emotional fences. This chapter will show you how to claim your emotional territory and protect it with better fences.

In order to claim your territory you must have a healthy sense of self. That means a sensitivity to, and respect for, your own health and well-being. If you are beset by guilt, you must learn that *your* needs and desires are just as important as anyone else's. That's not to say your needs and desires are more important than those of others, but they are equal to those of others. Getting to the place where you believe that and can act on it might be a quantum leap for you.

You will notice that this chapter has examples of how to do this step in each of the eight guilt-inducing situations. That is because claiming territory is the key step; I want to be sure you understand how to do it no matter what is behind your toxic guilt. The other steps are more general, and you will be able to apply them easily to any of the eight situations.

Language

Language is extremely important. The words you use create impressions and make things happen. The spoken word and the written word are your best tools for claiming territory, but if you are plagued by toxic guilt you may not even have language for claiming territory. Here are a few practical statements to prime the pump; you can memorize them so you'll be ready when it's time to start claiming territory:

- No, thank you.
- In order to take care of myself, I'll have to say no.
- Excuse me, but I was next.
- I'm sorry, but that won't work for me.
- This isn't what we agreed to.
- I'm not satisfied with that answer.
- May I please speak to your supervisor?
- I'm sorry, but that's more than I'm able (or willing) to do.
- I know you do not agree, but it is my decision.
- This is who I am.
- Thank you, but I think I'll pass.

Enmeshment: A Tender Trap

If you are besieged by guilt, you may be vulnerable to becoming enmeshed with others. That is because you probably have an exaggerated need for approval, and so you may allow others to take over your emotional terrain. Conversely, you may intrude on another person's psychological property if you have a heightened sense of responsibility. Since enmeshment is a personal territory issue, it merits discussion here.

Enmeshment is a psychological process that causes pain and conflict in intimate relationships. It can occur between spouses or lovers, between parents and children, or between close friends.

Human beings are drawn to intimacy with other people. We long to merge with another and "become one." We are also drawn to independence; we want to be our own person and stand on our own two feet. When intimacy is desired, we move toward the other person until some form of merging is experienced. (In the case of lovers, this involves sexual merging.) We celebrate feeling close to another for a while, but we can't stay there too long. The need to separate and be independent emerges, and we pull away.

The ebb and flow of movement toward and away from other people is part and parcel of our nature. In a healthy relationship, there is a balance between merging with the other person and moving away from the other person to claim our separateness. Enmeshment occurs when, in merging with another, the boundaries of our separateness get blurred. There is confusion about whose territory is whose.

Here's an example of the blurring of boundaries that occurs when one partner abdicates too much territory and the other person is over-responsible.

Regina and Skip's Story

Regina and Skip had a happy marriage. Skip felt lucky to have such a beautiful wife, and Regina felt safe with her loving, financially responsible husband. He was all she ever wanted. Skip was drawn to Regina's naiveté and childlike sweetness. Regina felt safe with Skip and thought of him as her knight in shining armor.

Skip harbored a deep-seated fear that Regina would find someone else. Why would such a beauty be content with an ordinary man like him? Conversely, Regina worried about her ability to hang on to her husband. Skip was a man of stellar character from a good family who was respected by the community; she was a woman of humble circumstances from a chaotic and broken home. The couple avoided conflict at all costs.

Regina was somewhat financially irresponsible. She refused to follow a budget and tended to overspend. She put off balancing the checkbook and occasionally was late paying the bills. Early in the marriage she and Skip had argued about it, and he took over managing the finances. Regina was relieved; it ended the conflict between them, and she didn't have to deal with the bill-paying process anymore.

As time went by, she allowed him to take more and more control over their finances. Finally, Skip took possession of the only checkbook and credit card. Regina had to ask his permission to use either of them when she needed something. Skip was pleased with the arrangement. Her dependence on him made him feel safer about their relationship. He also felt more secure when she was at home with the children rather than being out in the workforce, so he encouraged her to be a stay-at-home mom.

All went well for a few years; Skip liked the role of rescuer and protector, and Regina liked being rescued and protected. But over time, Regina began to resent the arrangement. She felt she was not an equal partner in the marriage, and she grew to resent her second-class status.

The kids were older now, and so Regina contemplated going back to work. Skip's response was to suggest that they have another baby. Regina was horrified. She longed to confront her husband about her dissatisfaction with the relationship, but she was too afraid of his disapproval. By the time she came to see me, she was considering leaving the marriage.

Analyzing Regina and Skip's Enmeshment

This story might not make much sense logically, but it makes perfect sense emotionally. Regina's heightened need to please her husband caused her to abdicate too much territory to him. Skip's insecurity and excessive sense of responsibility led him to intrude on his wife's personal space. Boundary confusion and enmeshment was the result.

In therapy the couple learned that insecurity about the other's affection and loyalty was at the heart of their trouble. Skip was afraid Regina would find someone else if she worked outside the home. Regina was afraid that if she stood up for herself and expressed her dissatisfaction about their financial arrangement—or anything else—Skip would resent her and leave the relationship.

When relationships become enmeshed, as Skip and Regina's had, the normal and usual process of separation and individuation can evoke feelings of rejection, fear, anger, and panic. When Skip and Regina were able to reassure each other about their loyalty and love, they began to relax and were much less suspicious and defensive.

Next, we tackled the boundary issues. Regina learned to stand up for herself and claim her territory, and Skip learned to identify whose property was whose. With boundaries established and respected, the relationship improved and the marriage survived.

When a therapist sees that a couple (or a parent and child) are enmeshed, the goal becomes helping them to establish boundaries, to define whose territory is whose, and to assist each person in claiming and maintaining their own territory.

Reclaiming Lost Territory

Claiming your territory in the first place takes courage. Reclaiming territory you once had, but lost, can be even more daunting. Perhaps you lost yourself in your marriage because your world revolved around your spouse. Maybe you gave too much of your emotional property to your children by allowing them to become the sole focus of your life. Possibly a close friend slowly but surely took control of the relationship and started making all the decisions.

If you allow other people, even people you greatly care about, to step over your flattened fences and come and go as they please on your land, you will probably end up resenting them. It can be a rude awakening to discover that intruders have possession of your property.

Years ago, I attended a group for spouses in a substance-abuse rehab center where my (now ex) husband was a patient. The group facilitator began the first session by asking each participant to introduce himself or herself and share something that had nothing to do with their spouse (who was in treatment).

The leader said, "Just talk about you. Tell us what you like. Talk about your hobbies and interests. Share your dreams for the future."

It was an easy enough assignment, but when my turn came, I couldn't think of a thing—not one thing. It was not until that moment that I realized how consumed I had become with the care and maintenance of my husband. I could have said a lot about *his* hobbies, interests, and dreams!

I see many clients who lose themselves in their marriages as I once did. Wanting to please or help, or simply keep the peace, well-meaning husbands and wives devote more and more time and attention to their spouse until there is nothing left for them.

Claiming Territory and Leaving a Relationship

Sometimes the only way to claim your territory is to leave a relationship. If you have tried everything you know and your boundaries are still not respected, you may not have another choice. It only takes one person to end a relationship. If your emotional survival is at stake—and perhaps the emotional survival of your children—I hope you have the strength and the good sense to pull up stakes and get out.

Margie's Story

Margie was part of a work team in a large corporation. Team meetings, conference calls, and seminars were the order of the day. Margie's husband, Dan, was the jealous type, and after seven years of marriage, Margie was sick of his suspicions and insecurities. Peter, a colleague on her team, seemed to have everything Dan was in short supply of—maturity, self-confidence, a sense of humor, and a sympathetic ear.

When Margie and Peter stopped at the hotel lounge for a drink after the first day of the sales conference, she found herself spilling her frustration and disillusionment all over the small cocktail table where they sat. Peter was attentive and responsive. More than that, he seemed to take her seriously, something Dan never did.

"That was the beginning," Margie told me in our first session.

"The beginning of what?" I queried.

"The beginning of me realizing what I was missing."

Margie was attracted to Peter, and she thought the feeling was mutual, but they were both married. Margie wasn't about to "go there," as she said. She sought my counsel because she wanted to either improve her marriage or find a way to leave it.

Over the next few months she and Dan met with me weekly. Margie was honest with Dan and told him she had discussed private matters about their relationship with Peter. She acknowledged that she had been wrong to do so, apologized, and said it wouldn't happen again. Explaining that she wanted things to be better between them, she begged him to put the "Peter thing" aside so they could move forward.

Dan was either unable or unwilling to let the emotional betrayal go. He suspected Peter and Margie were up to something, and he became an amateur private investigator. He followed her, taped phone conversations, and interrogated her friends and colleagues.

When it became apparent that the dynamics of their relationship were not changing, Margie requested an individual session. She told me that because of Peter she had learned what a truly emotionally intimate relationship was. She felt more emotionally connected to Peter than she had ever been to Dan. She did not intend to pursue a romantic relationship with Peter, but she wanted someone like him, someone with whom she could safely bare her soul, someone who was mature and secure. Racked with guilt, she wondered if she would ever have the courage to leave Dan.

Couple sessions were painful. Dan was angry and accused his wife of being frigid. Margie acknowledged that for the past few months, she had not been able to bring herself to have sex with her husband. She tried to appease him in every other way, but of course, he wanted a sexual expression of her affection.

Her guilt was so overwhelming, and she was so afraid of hurting him, that she couldn't articulate the truth; there was nothing wrong with her sex drive, she just had lost all desire for *him*. Because she hung in, he hung on, hoping things would change. It was like watching a slow, painful death.

Finally, exhausted, frustrated, and at her wits' end, Margie phoned to ask me to help her overcome her guilt so she could leave the marriage and move on. We worked on claiming her territory in individual sessions, and over time Margie came to see that she had a right to happiness—that her happiness was as important as Dan's. Her relationship with Peter had given her a vision of intimacy that she'd never experienced and a dream of possibilities for the future. In the end, feeling sad but resolute, she told Dan that their marriage was over.

Claiming Territory and Hanging In

Claiming territory doesn't always mean leaving the relationship. It may mean saving it. The resentment that builds over time when you slowly but surely abdicate your territory to your partner or spouse is deadly. But take heart; it may not be too late to turn things around. Changing such a pattern may mean traversing extremely difficult emotional terrain, but the destination may be worth it.

Do not undertake such a journey without proper equipment and a good compass. Take one measured step at a time. If you take off in a rush, you may tire well before the end is in sight. Giant leaps can result in landing flat on your face.

Begin by claiming your territory in small ways. If your husband makes all the decisions and you have been quietly acquiescing, perhaps for years, begin claiming territory in small matters first. If he wants chops for dinner and you would like to make meatloaf, start there. Say something like, "I know you wanted chops, but I needed to use the hamburger. Anyway, I thought meatloaf sounded good for tonight." If he protests, quietly but firmly hold your ground. (Please note that I do *not* recommend this approach if your husband is abusive!)

When you have accomplished standing up for yourself in a small way, move to the next level. If he makes vacation plans for the beach every year and you love the mountains, claim your territory. "We've gone to the beach for three years in a row. I've enjoyed every year of it, but this year it's my turn. I want to go to the mountains. Here's what I propose . . ." And stick to it.

Expect stormy weather (which we'll talk more about in the next chapter). Determine to hold your territory, even if it means going to the mountains by yourself. Remember, the resentment that builds inside of you from not claiming your territory can destroy the relationship.

The following story illustrates how one man was able to claim his territory and resurrect his marriage.

Brian's Story

Brian was a pleasant, affable guy. Gray-haired and fit for his forty-four years, he started the session by saying, "My attorney sent me. She doesn't think I know what I want, and she's right!" He laughed self-consciously.

Married to his second wife for six years, Brian was contemplating divorce and had visited an attorney to explore his legal options. His health was suffering. He was constantly on edge, had tension headaches, and high blood pressure. His doctor thought it was his work. It wasn't.

Brian explained that he thought he'd chosen carefully the second time around. He and Becky had been together for five years before they got married. But it had all gone wrong.

Becky was a pretty woman, he told me, and a spoiled only child. She was conscientious about her physical appearance and worked out every day. As far as he could tell, that was about all she did.

She had become more and more demanding as the years went by. She wanted his time, she wanted his money, and she wanted everything her way. She was always right, and always wronged—a convincing victim. Brian, a peacemaker by nature, let things slide, looked the other way, and acquiesced most of the time.

Now he sat in my office, shocked and appalled by how much territory he had relinquished to his wife. He was also aware that as he lost parts of himself to her, he was losing his affection for her as well.

Things changed when Brian began to pull away. Becky knew something was wrong and did a 180. She was suddenly sweet, attentive, and affectionate: the girl he married. But he couldn't trust that it would last. I suggested we do some couple work.

Brian had allowed his wife free access to his emotional property; he had fences to mend. As we moved forward in therapy, he started standing up for himself and learned to manage the resulting conflict. In turn, Becky had more respect for him.

As he learned to claim his territory, the resentment he felt for Becky began to dissipate. Now he had no reason to punish her (in a passive-aggressive manner) by putting things off and procrastinating. She was delighted in the change and began to show her appreciation in tangible ways. In the end, the marriage survived.

Claiming Territory with Children

When children are young, the territory between parent and child is shared. As they grow and develop, it is the parents' responsibility to help them carve out their own territory and build fences. In that process, parents and children should learn to respect one another's personal space.

As a general rule, parents have more right to trespass on their children's property than the other way around. For example, parents have the right to listen in on phone calls and go through their children's backpacks if they suspect their child is in danger (from drugs, self-harm, and so on).

Many well-meaning parents do not set proper boundaries with their children because they don't want to make them mad or disappoint them. However, enforcing boundaries with children is good for them and good for their parents. If you have allowed your children too much access to your personal territory, you may need to think about establishing clear boundaries and repairing your fences. I have a story from Mother Nature that may give you that extra boost of confidence you need.

The Ducks' Story!

My parents live on a cove. The cove is an inlet, much like the web between the thumb and the forefinger of the hand. Their house is close to the water, and they have been watching waterfowl there for more than twenty years. There is predictability in the family life of the mallards, swans, and Canada geese who are homesteaders in what is virtually my parents' front yard.

In the spring, a bird couple locates a good nesting place, usually a protected spot in a crevice of the jagged bluffs across the cove from the house. The mother mallard lays her eggs and her mate swims patrol in the water nearby. He also forages for food and brings home supper. When the eggs hatch, the proud parents show off their brood to those of us who sit on the deck and watch. Back and forth they swim in a line, Dad in the lead, then Mom, then the little ones. As if to give the humans on the deck an even closer look, the parents march their babies up the incline to the house, hovering around them protectively as the tiny balls of fluff explore the yard, pecking at the ground and stumbling over sticks or acorns.

Some weeks later another show begins. The heretofore attentive, protective parents decide that it's time for their lanky, ill-mannered adolescents to get a life of their own. The offspring aren't at all interested in such a notion. Leaving their cushy home is not in their game plan, and they resist the relocation project by relentlessly clinging to their parents. A power struggle ensues.

At some point, the parents decide enough is enough. Partly running, partly swimming, and partly flying, the parents, squawking loudly and spewing water, run at their youngsters until the disbelieving brood gets the message. One by one, the astonished young adults swim away.

We can learn a lot from these wild waterfowl. The parents are clear about their boundaries; they are in charge of their brood and assume responsibility for nurturing, protecting, and teaching them. With those tasks completed, the parents launch their young into adulthood with dispatch and without apologies.

I advise parents who have teenagers to survey their situation and repair or reinforce damaged fences before the kids leave home. Young people do astonishingly well when they know the boundaries. The following statements (or variations on them) are fair and helpful:

- We will finance four years of college—no more.
- We will pay for tuition, books, and residence-hall fees; the rest is up to you.
- We can only afford tuition and books; the rest is up to you.
- If you don't make at least a 3.0 grade-point average, you're on your own. No more money.
- College is on us. Grad school is on you.
- If you flunk out of college, you can live at home for three months; then you have to move out.

- If you lose a job or get a divorce, you can move home for three months; then you have to move out.
- We will not be able to pay for a wedding.
- We can give you a set amount of money for your wedding.
- We will bail you out of jail one time—that's once in your lifetime.
- If you ever wind up in jail, you're on your own.

Your potential for guilt is greatly reduced when your kids know the boundaries ahead of time.

When parents bail their kids out of every messy situation in life, they send a clear message: *we don't believe you are capable of managing this on your own, so we'll do it for you.* It is difficult for a young person to develop any sense of managing his or her own territory when parents climb over or crawl under their fences. It is trespassing, after all.

Claiming Territory with Rules—the Basics

If your children are still living at home and you are sick and tired of them running roughshod over your territory, it is time to act. Sit down with your spouse (if you are single, you have my respect and compassion—it's a tough job at best and a tougher one when you're on your own!) and decide what you want the house rules to be. Get a large sheet of paper and divide it into two columns: rules on the left, penalties for breaking them on the right. Try to make the consequences match the rule if you can.

Keep it simple; five to ten rules should do it. List only the basics. It's easy to overdo your list of tasks or expectations and make it too confusing. Then you will feel overwhelmed trying to enforce the rules and give up. Your paper might look something like this if your kids are preteens:

House Rules

Rules	Penalties
1. Beds made by 7 A.M.	1. Time-out in room after school for 30 minutes and make bed
2. All homework done before 8 P.M.	2. No computer time for two days
3. Trash emptied every Wednesday	3. Allowance docked $1.00
4. Bedrooms straightened on Saturday	4. Lose video games for weekend

Announce the rules with a flourish and post them on the refrigerator door. When the kids mess up and must suffer the consequences, it's not your fault—it's the *rule's* fault. You're sorry, but what can you do?

Of course you will want to modify the rules as your kids get older. Here's an example of what the rules might look like for teens:

House Rules

Rules	Penalties
1. Midnight curfew on weekends	1. Grounded the next weekend night
2. No grades below a B	2. No cell phone after 5 P.M. for one month
3. Trash emptied every Wednesday	3. Allowance docked $3.00
4. Bedrooms straightened and sheets washed on Saturday	4. Lose car for two days

Note that the consequences are specific. Do not say "no cell phone"—it's way too vague. But "no cell phone after 5 P.M. for one month" is clear. There is a beginning and an end, and everybody knows exactly what will happen.

Here is a slick trick for tracking curfews: if the curfew is midnight, set an alarm clock for midnight and place it where you will hear it if it goes off (in the hall or on the kitchen table—certainly not in your bedroom). Instruct your teens to turn the alarm off when they come home. If the alarm goes off and you wake up, they're busted!

If your kids are still living at home, the key to claiming territory is good boundaries that are consistently enforced. You can do it!

Claiming Territory with Parents

It's never too late to claim your territory back from your parents, but it's seldom easy. In order to do it, you must risk upsetting them, hurting their feelings, and making them mad at you. The challenge is claiming your territory while staying in a relationship with them. You can control your part in this by being honest and loving, but you can't control your parents' response.

Marsha's Story

Marsha, a fifty-one-year-old church secretary, sought therapy after she lost her job. In addition to being devastated by being fired, she complained of generalized aching in her body, diminished energy, and loss of interest in almost everything. The depression inventory she filled out in my office indicated that she was clinically depressed, and I suggested she see her physician for a thorough checkup. Her medical doctor diagnosed fibromyalgia and depression. The doctor prescribed antidepressant medication and sent her to a fibromyalgia clinic for treatment.

Marsha, who had never married, was the primary caregiver for her elderly mother, a widow who lived in a small town fifty miles away. She said her eighty-seven-year-old mother had always been domineering, controlling, and critical. When Mother said "Jump," everyone jumped.

Marsha, the oldest of three siblings, had felt responsible for her mother's happiness ever since she could remember. Scoffing, she said, "I don't know why I keep trying to please her—I never have and I never will!"

It didn't take long to discover that Marsha had devoted most of her life to her mother. The only territory she claimed for herself was her work. "My work was my life," she said, weeping. "And now it's gone."

With her work taken away from her, Marsha realized she had nothing to call her own but a strong faith in God, and that did not feel like enough. Shocked and grief-stricken about her loss, she turned to therapy for help.

Step One was to confess the reality of her mother's encroachment on her life. The confession came pouring out. Attempting to please her mother and feeling responsible for her mother's happiness all her life had been emotionally expensive indeed. Marsha was coming to understand that she had never felt she had the right to her own emotions. She resented her mother for taking over her life, and she resented herself for letting it happen.

Step Two was for Marsha to begin claiming her territory. The goal of our work was to find a way for her to be connected to her mother in a healthy manner.

Marsha's mother was in poor health, and Marsha and her siblings had arranged twenty-four-hour in-home care for their mother. Knowing that in time the money for such an expensive solution would run out, the siblings approached their mother about the prospect of placement in a nursing home (a less costly option). Their mother would have no part of such a plan.

Marsha came to my office in a panic. "I know what will happen." She fidgeted with the throw pillow on the sofa, picking at the fringe. "My whole life savings—what retirement I've earned, my investments, everything—will end up being spent on my mother, and I'll never get my dream!"

"Your dream?"

"I've wanted to own a bed-and-breakfast for years. I always stay in them when I travel, and everything about owning one intrigues me. It would fit me perfectly—I know it. I've been saving with the hope that when I retire I can make my dream come true."

"Why would you spend all your savings on your mother when you have your dream?"

"I'd have to."

"Your mother has some money and owns her home, right?"

"Yes."

"You have siblings, right?"

"Yes."

She still looked panic-stricken. "Do you want to pay for your mother's care?" I asked.

"Oh, no!" she cried in dismay.

I could see there was something else. When I probed further, I learned that Marsha feared her own guilt. When push came to shove, she thought guilt would cause her to cave in and use her savings for her mother. She talked about her guilt as if it were something beyond her control—a force outside her body with a will of its own.

Marsha felt entirely responsible for her mother's care. After all, she reasoned, her mother was a widow, old and alone, and Marsha did not have a husband or family to care for. I suggested it would be different if her mother were destitute or truly alone—but she wasn't. There appeared to be ample funds to support her mother in an extended-care facility, and Marsha had two siblings living nearby.

"But honoring your father and mother is a religious commandment," she argued, "one of the Ten Commandments." What else could she do? She felt that if she weren't willing to finance her mother's care at home, she wasn't honoring her. I pointed out that there are many ways to honor a person and that "honoring" didn't necessarily require Marsha to deplete her life savings.

In a few weeks Marsha was ready to claim her territory. We devised a plan. She told her sister and brother that she was not able to contribute any more funds toward their mother's long-term care than she already was. She also created a document illustrating the cost of home health care versus nursing-home costs. Then she speculated the gross amount of their mother's estate, including monies from the sale of her house. Her mother could afford a nursing home for a number of years.

Her siblings were not pleased; they had been counting on Marsha to come through as she always had. Marsha held her ground, and after a few scratchy encounters her brother and sister backed off.

Marsha's mother might not get to live out her life in her own home as she wishes, but Marsha is no longer panicked that, once again, guilt will cause her to do something she doesn't want to do. Now that she feels secure in her decision not to abdicate any more territory—emotional or financial—to her mother, she is free to be as supportive and loving to her mother as she possibly can.

Eventually, Marsha found a job as a school secretary, and she now spends some of her free time researching the bed-and-breakfast industry on the Internet.

Claiming Territory When You Are a Captive of Your Religious Community

When religious obligations, activities, and beliefs dictate the course of your life and you feel like a prisoner to them, your territory is under siege. It is one thing to be a faithful follower of your religious tradition; it is another to be controlled by it in an unhealthy way. When you find yourself responding to the needs and dictates of your religious community whether you want to or not, it is time to take action.

Please note that I am not saying there is anything inherently wrong with responding to the obligations, activities, and dictates of your religious community; for many people, this is the most important and satisfying aspect of their lives. But there is a problem if you feel guilty when you don't say yes to every need and dictate that comes along. It is also a problem if you feel crushing guilt because you do not agree with the prevailing opinion of your religious community.

The complicating aspect of a religious community is that people often place the authority of the community over a relationship with God. For example, attendance at religious services on Sunday can be so emphasized by a religious community that people feel guilty if they go on a camping trip over the weekend. Perhaps being close to nature, and leaving the obligations of life behind now and then, will provide a space for God to enter that would not be available in the pew of a church.

Not long ago, I attended services in a local church as a guest. All went well until the preacher launched into a diatribe about certain candidates in an upcoming state election. I did not agree with the preacher's choices on any level, and I wondered if members of the congregation who also disagreed with their pastor's selections might feel guilty about it. Then I wondered if there were those who would feel too guilty to disagree at all.

Claiming territory with your religious community may mean you must speak out with a dissenting voice, or it may mean you have to leave.

Peggy's Story

Peggy grew up in a devout family where church was the central focus of family life. Sunday services, Wednesday night bible study for the adults and youth group for the children, and

Thursday choir practice created the rhythm of the week. Peggy loved it all.

When she went away to college she became a member of her faith tradition's campus ministry. She also took some courses in women's studies. She learned about the role of women in American culture and about the evolution of women's rights. She learned about the plight of women around the world, especially in underdeveloped countries. And in the context of these classes, she learned about herself.

Slowly but surely it dawned on her that there was a grave injustice in her faith tradition. Women were not allowed any positions of authority in her church. They could not become pastors, serve on church boards, or hold office. She was dismayed.

Peggy was not one to question authority or raise a dissenting voice. She was a rule-follower and people-pleaser. But this time, sitting in silence was more painful than confronting the guilt she would feel if she stepped out of line.

Peggy was ready to claim territory. She questioned her campus minister about her church's treatment of women. She also interrogated her pastor when she went home for semester break. She got no satisfactory answers. Her parents' rationale was equally insufficient; it's always been that way, they said.

With a great deal of pain, but also with resolve, Peggy decided she could not continue to be a member of a religious community that disparaged women. She told her parents of her distress and sadly left her religious community. Sometimes claiming territory is painful and there is loss involved.

Claiming Territory When You Want to Move or Change Jobs

Life is not a dress rehearsal. We've heard this saying so often it's lost its meaning and impact. We relegate our response to

"Oh, right" and dismiss the hard truth of the words. Part of that response is denial of our own mortality—we don't really believe this is it.

If your best friend wanted to move to get a fresh start, or leave a job that was crushing her spirit, you'd probably encourage her to take the step. "Life is not a dress rehearsal," you'd say. But when we guilty types are faced with such an option ourselves, we have a zillion reasons why we can't act on our desires.

You can find the courage to claim your territory when you want to move or change jobs by following these three guidelines:

1. Seek the company of people who support your plan. Maximize your contact with those who would encourage you in your plan and avoid those who would not. If people who are close to you will not, or do not, support your idea, don't discuss it with them. You may even need to reduce contact with them for a while.

2. Focus on what you say to yourself in your own head. Listen to yourself: if you tell yourself this place or this job is killing you, pay attention and take it seriously—maybe it is. If you focus your attention on something, it will grow. If you dwell on what scares you about what you want to do or obsess about the guilt you'll feel, the fear and guilt will become bigger and stronger than your resolve to make a change.

When you catch yourself thinking negative thoughts, try thought-blocking. Imagine a large red octagon-shaped stop sign: STOP.

3. Examine the evidence of your own abilities. Where have you been successful? For example, have you reached some academic goals? Have you made a place for yourself in your community or in your job, even if you don't like it? Do you have some successful relationships—with friends? Family? A partner? What have you

survived—a divorce or a personal loss? Then you are a survivor, and you can prevail in this new challenge.

My Husband's Story

My husband was trapped in the wrong place and in the wrong job when he was a young man. He grew up in a rural community where his parents were poor farmers. They did not share his desires for higher education; in fact, they were against it. Their goal for him after high school was a good job and active participation on the family farm. But he had other aspirations.

He told me how proud his family was when he secured a job selling major appliances following his high school graduation. He did well in his job, but his spirit shriveled. He wanted to go to college; he longed to get away.

My husband was fortunate to find a mentor. A physician in town took an interest in him, encouraged him in his dream for higher education, and provided a loan to make the dream a reality. My husband was elated, but he felt so guilty about leaving his parents and the farm that he almost missed the opportunity of his life. The internal turmoil he experienced was nearly paralyzing.

Finally, knowing that staying in his hometown was killing him, and believing he could succeed in college, he made the break. But months passed before he could bring himself to go home to visit his family. He knew he was letting his parents down, and the guilt he felt was overwhelming; facing them was more than he could bear.

The story has a happy ending. My husband went on from college to law school and has been a judge most of his professional life. He continued to have a close and positive relationship with his parents, who were ultimately proud of his success.

Claiming Territory with Controlling Family Members

If you feel like a volleyball bounced from one side of the court to the other, or a cherry pie carefully divided into equal sections, it may be time to claim your territory from your relatives.

There are in-laws and divorced biological parents who scrutinize the comings and goings of their adult children as closely as obsessed baseball fans monitor the ERAs and RBIs of every major-league team. If a family spent three and a half days of last summer's vacation with her parents, they'd better spend three and a half days with his parents this summer!

Ryan and Monica's Story

I'll remind you of Ryan and Monica from Chapter 12. The couple was pulled between their parents; Ryan's mother kept score of how often and how long the couple and their children visited Monica's parents and then demanded equal time.

After several sessions with the couple, I asked Ryan to come in for an individual session. Ryan told me that although he loved his parents and felt guilty about his true desires, he would really much rather spend time with Monica's family. However, he wanted to do the right thing; he wanted to honor his parents by having a good relationship with them. Ryan had completed Step One, Speak the Truth.

Monica's individual session was similar. She respected her in-laws and wanted to foster the relationship between them and the children, but she had had it with forced marches just to even the score. She was furious at Ryan for blaming her when the scales tipped in favor of more time with her parents, when she knew he would rather be visiting her parents than his own. She confessed to feeling that Ryan was weak because he wasn't strong enough to stand up to his mother. Monica had completed Step One as well.

In my next session with both Ryan and Monica, I facilitated an honest discussion between them, and they told each other the real reasons why they were each feeling miserable. It was time for Step Two. The couple's homework for the next session was to brainstorm ways that Ryan could claim his territory from his parents.

When I saw them the next week, they brought the results of their work on paper. Ryan would have a serious talk with his mother and say:

- that he loved his parents deeply, and he loved Monica's parents too
- that his mother's record-keeping of time spent with Monica's parents versus time spent with them was causing pain and distress in his family
- that it was time to stop the game-playing
- that in the future, Ryan and his family would spend some holidays at their own home

They had done a great job. I only had two additional suggestions. I thought that Ryan might remind his mother that you cannot measure love, that it is an infinite commodity in the human condition and there is plenty to go around for everyone. I also wondered aloud why Ryan and Monica were required to tell their parents (on either side) where they were going, or when, or for how long. That is a territory issue too. Every couple gets to close and lock the gate to their territory at times. Privacy is a right.

Remember, good fences make good neighbors; establishing clear boundaries is the road to freedom. The words that we use are very important, because emotional fences are built with words. Choose them carefully. Here is some language that might help you claim your territory with controlling relatives.

- We love you and want to be with you whenever we can, but we have to be fair to everybody and take care of ourselves. So this Hanukkah . . .
- This year we're starting our own tradition around the holidays.
- This Christmas we need to work on strengthening our own family unit because we work so much. We'd love for you to join us (at such-and-such a time).
- This Thanksgiving we've decided to work on strengthening our own family unit by spending the day together. Since we can't be with you, we'd like to arrange a special day together during the holiday time.

Claiming Territory When You Want to Come Out

The very act of coming out *is* claiming territory. Claiming your sexual identity is a proclamation of who you are. It is also a proclamation of ownership—this is me and I am owning it. When, where, and to whom one wants to come out is a personal decision and should be considered carefully and thoughtfully. Some people are very private about who they come out to, usually because they harbor some guilt about it or because they know their livelihood would be at stake (due to prejudice in the workplace or due to the nature of their career). Others do their best to make sure everyone knows they are gay or lesbian.

People must be seen, heard, and experienced for who they really are in order to have optimal emotional health; it is not possible for that to happen if you are gay or lesbian and pretending to be heterosexual.

If you are gay or lesbian and are still not out, I am sure you have very good reasons for it. One of the reasons is bound to be toxic guilt. If working through your guilt could set you free, then claiming territory and coming out—even if it is to just one person—might be a necessary beginning. I do suggest using caution and going slowly in coming out; I have seen people claim their sexual identity to themselves and become so overjoyed and elated that they want the whole world to know. It can be devastating to discover that the whole world may not be warm and accepting.

Ling's Story

Ling's grandparents immigrated to the United States from China and joined other family members in the restaurant business. Her father was born in the States; he learned everything there was to know about operating the restaurant, from cooking to catering. He went to college, majored in business, and met Ling's mother, also Chinese. By the time Ling was born, the modest little restaurant had grown into a lucrative empire. There were three restaurants locally and eleven statewide.

Ling's family was affluent and well known in the community. They were respected for their philanthropy and support of local nonprofit agencies and endeavors. The family was active in their church, where Ling's mother sang in the choir.

Ling excelled in sports and was popular in her group of friends. She seemed happy and carefree until her sophomore year in high school. By the middle of the year, she had dropped out of youth group at church and quit the volleyball team. Her grades went down, and she began isolating herself from old friends. Her mother was alarmed and called me.

When I first saw Ling, I was struck by the way she was dressed. Although slightly built, she wore baggy pants and an oversized tee as if to hide her body. Part of her long dark hair was pulled back into a ponytail and loose, thick portions drooped around her face. She wore no makeup. I wondered if she was intentionally making herself as unattractive as possible.

We'd been meeting for several weeks when Ling told me that she thought she was a lesbian. She'd been attracted to females for as long as she could remember but tried to ignore her feelings and go on with life. Everything changed when she started high school, though. Her girlfriends were getting boyfriends and talking about it. Conversations about boys and sex were the order of the day in her peer group, but she had no interest in boys. Also, she found herself in the company of girls at school who were out as lesbians and open about it, which left her feeling both envious and slightly disgusted. Her attraction to girls had only increased with age, but her guilt about it increased as well.

None of the girls in her group of friends appeared to be on the same page, so she dared not talk to them. Talking to her parents was out of the question. She was very close to both of them, but they were traditional and she was their only daughter. Her older brother might have been an appropriate confidant, but he was away at college. Her response was to pull in. It was better to lose herself in music and the Internet than to deal with her churning emotions. However, Ling had now taken the first step—she had confessed the reality of her life to me.

In the nonjudgmental environment of my office, it became easier for Ling to relax the judgment she had against herself and explore her feelings. She talked about her first real crush on a girl in sixth grade and how brokenhearted she was when the girl moved away. With some light in her face, she told me about a girl at school who had caught her eye and whom she knew to be a lesbian. Ling felt certain she was gay, but she was trapped by guilt, unable to share her life with anyone but a therapist for one hour a week.

With a lot of caution and with no pressure, I introduced Step Two. If Ling wanted to claim territory by coming out to someone she trusted, I would help her. I wondered aloud if that someone could be her mother. Thus, the conversation began.

We explored every possibility. Ling was secure in her relationship with her mother but fearful of disappointing her. The guilt of not being the girl her mother wished for was hard to bear. But then again, her mother had always supported her. I pointed out that her mother knew something was wrong, or she would not have contacted me.

We talked about how sad Ling was not to be able to share this important subject with her mother. She told me about her fear of coming out and how she dreaded the inevitable rejection that would follow. Finally, Ling decided to tell her mother. We roleplayed the conversation so that she could practice how she would introduce the subject and what she would say.

One night a week or so later, when Ling was alone with her mother, she did it. Her mother was loving and supportive. Ling was her daughter, she said, and her sexual identity did not change the way she felt about her. The next day Ling, with her mother at her side, came out to her father. He was loving and supportive as well. Ling was surprised when her mother suggested they talk to their pastor, but she agreed to a meeting. The pastor was warm and reassuring. Although Ling didn't know it, there were several gay members of their church and they were welcome as brothers and sisters.

When Ling came out to a few select friends and was accepted and supported, she began to change. She started dressing fashionably and took care with her hair. She even began to wear makeup. Her grades went up and she signed up for track. In short, she blossomed.

Claiming her sexual identity reversed a downward spiral in Ling's life and restored her sense of self. The last time she was in my office I overheard her talking to her mom on her cell phone. "No kidding!" she said, her face bright and animated. "I've become a magnet for chicks!"

Claiming Territory with an Unplanned Pregnancy

An unplanned and unwanted pregnancy brings many women the most difficult experience of their lives. The panic, anger, remorse, and shame can be overwhelming. Some women are immobilized by guilt; they have no idea how to stake out—much less claim— their territory. They do not even know whether their lives, bodies, emotions, health, and financial concerns are private or public property.

Claiming one's own personal territory in this situation is essential. It is the woman's life, the woman's body, and the woman's choice. I advise a woman with an unwanted pregnancy to examine every option and then decide what is in her best interest. If terminating a pregnancy is against all her personal religious convictions, then doing so would probably not be in her best interest. If, however, she wants to terminate the pregnancy, but the fear of God's wrath or the church's wrath has her stuck in her tracks, there is work to do. A fear-based choice is no choice at all.

Kaitlyn's Story

Kaitlyn was only fourteen when she got pregnant. She lived in a small rural community where there was almost no racial diversity and plenty of prejudice. She was in love with Lamont, her African-American classmate; they had been keeping their relationship a secret from her family. Now she was pregnant.

Kaitlyn lived with her mother and two younger sisters. Her parents were divorced, and she saw her father regularly for visits. Her dad had remarried and had an infant son with his new wife. Now there was a looming problem: Kaitlyn's dad, unsophisticated and uneducated, was woefully prejudiced.

Kaitlyn was so guilty and afraid that she kept her pregnancy a secret from everyone. She felt guilty because good girls don't get pregnant in the first place, and they sure don't get pregnant by black boys. She was afraid because she knew her father would blame her mother for not having been a good enough parent. She was also afraid because she didn't know what her father would do to Lamont. So she told no one, and time passed.

Kaitlyn's mother eventually put two and two together and confronted her daughter about her suspicion. Kaitlyn confessed all, and her mother, although terribly afraid for her child, responded with love and support.

Kaitlyn's mother was a waitress in a local diner and also did shift work at the shoe factory in town just to make ends meet. When her mother was working, Kaitlyn was in charge of her two sisters. Her mom blamed herself for her daughter's pregnancy. If she could have been at home more often to supervise the girls, she felt this would not have happened.

By the time Kaitlyn's mother found out about her daughter's pregnancy, the options had diminished. Kaitlyn was too far along to terminate the pregnancy. When her mother told her father their daughter was pregnant, he blew up. He yelled and raged and blamed Kaitlyn's mother, as Kaitlyn had predicted he would. He called Kaitlyn every name in the book and banished her from his house.

At this point, Kaitlyn had basically two choices. She could keep her baby, or she could give her baby up for adoption. Kaitlyn's mother contacted a social services agency for assistance, and her caseworker recommended therapy.

Kaitlyn, a shy strawberry blonde with a sprinkling of freckles across her nose, was about six months pregnant when I met her. Her mother attended the session as well, explaining that my job was to help Kaitlyn decide what to do with her baby. Her mother thought she should keep her baby and was quite willing to help her daughter raise the child. Kaitlyn wondered about adoption.

I met with Kaitlyn on a weekly basis after that. She was paralyzed by guilt. She felt guilty that she was pregnant, guilty that she was upsetting her mother's life (which was difficult enough already), guilty that she was so bad that her father disowned her, and guilty that she was stupid enough to get herself in such a mess.

She was afraid she would lose Lamont as well, because he blamed her for getting pregnant. Her fantasy was that she and Lamont would get married and live happily ever after. But neither of them were even old enough to get driver's licenses! Kaitlyn's fantasy disappeared for good when she found out Lamont was interested in another girl at school.

When Kaitlyn and I talked about keeping the baby versus adoption, she was more and more in favor of adoption. Her mother pressured her to keep the baby, but Kaitlyn knew she did not have the life skills to rear a child and didn't want her mother to do it for her. We arranged a meeting with her caseworker, and Kaitlyn learned about traditional versus open adoptions. In the open-adoption process, the birth mother and the adoptive parents participate in the child's life. She knew right away that this was what she wanted to do.

Her mother balked. How could such an arrangement work? But Kaitlyn was resolute. When she claimed her territory and stood her ground, her mother backed off.

The adoptive parents were from another state and were looking for a biracial child. A meeting was arranged between them and Kaitlyn. They were lovely people, so supportive and encouraging that Kaitlyn felt confident she was doing the right thing. Kaitlyn and the adoptive parents corresponded throughout the pregnancy, and they were present at the baby's birth.

Kaitlyn's mother supported her daughter's decision in the end, and miraculously her father appeared at the hospital, playing the role of a doting grandparent. When the time came, it was not easy for Kaitlyn to let her baby go. But knowing the decision was hers made the loss tolerable.

Claiming territory is the key step to escaping toxic guilt. If you forget everything else, remember Step Two. If you don't learn to claim what is rightfully yours, you will continue to be trapped by guilt. When you have made up your mind to claim territory and stand your ground, you are well on your way to freedom. In Chapter 17 you will learn what to expect next and how to prepare for it.

17

Step Three:
Brace for the Storm

Frequent flyers on guilt trips usually struggle with this step. The guilt-ridden do not want storms. They do not like to make waves, they do not want to hurt people, and they certainly do not want anyone to think ill of them. No wonder they are lousy at building fences and claiming their territory—but it has to be done.

Expectations and Preparations

When you begin to claim or reclaim your personal territory, people probably will not like it much. Folks are used to you giving in, abdicating control, and taking care of them. Claiming your territory and asserting yourself will be new behavior. You will surprise, maybe shock, and even anger some people. But bracing for the storm means you batten down the emotional hatches and do what you need to do, regardless of the furor it may cause.

It is possible to tolerate the disapproval of other people, whether it's temporary or permanent. This is an important point, because disapproval can seem unbearable to chronically guilty people. If Aunt Sally, or a colleague, or a friend, or even just an acquaintance is displeased, it can feel like your emotional survival is at stake. It is an illogical fear, of course, but emotionally it feels very real. Remember, for some guilt-ridden people, identity itself is tied to pleasing others. Learning to tolerate other people's disappointment or displeasure is an important step along the road to recovery from toxic guilt.

In order to take care of yourself and balance your life, you may need to (lovingly) tell the truth: *I am sorry, but I think this relationship has run its course. I know this will create a change that will be hard for you, but I am quitting my job. I'd love to do lunch another day; today I need to stay home. Could we talk about this later; I'm really busy right now.* Stand your ground, even if it hurts someone you care about or makes them mad at you.

In this chapter I will focus on bracing for the storm when you are claiming territory and leaving a committed relationship, when you are claiming territory with children, and when you are claiming territory with a parent, because these situations are so common and are fraught with such pain and uncertainty. If you are bracing for the storm in a committed relationship but not leaving it, or are bracing for the storm with controlling family members, or are bracing for the storm with an unwanted pregnancy or coming out, your pain is no less great. You will find that the principles discussed here will apply to your situation just fine.

Bracing for the Storm in a Committed Relationship

When claiming territory means you must leave a relationship, the storm that follows can be horrific. You may have good reason to fear the onslaught. Overcoming the agony of hurting, wounding, and causing pain to the other person is bad enough, but there may be other consequences. Hurt and pain can turn into retribution. Movies like *Sleeping with the Enemy* and *Fatal Attraction* document the lengths to which a rejected partner can go. Even when physical aggression has not previously characterized the relationship, the potential for violence can be very real and it's wise to be cautious.

The litigation process can generate another kind of brutality. The decision to divorce is usually unilateral: one spouse wants out and the other wants to keep the marriage. The jilted partner often institutes lengthy and unnecessary legal action against the partner who leaves, as a way to seek revenge; sometimes the jilted partner disparages the character of the partner who leaves in an attempt to destroy his or her reputation. Hell hath no fury like a partner scorned. Bracing for the storm means a willingness to endure the worst of what you imagine might happen in order to find freedom.

Guilt over splitting up the family and fear of retaliation kept Elle in her marriage for far too long. Her domineering husband had all the money and all the power—there was no telling what he would do if she left him. With a good deal of preparation and the support of family, friends, and therapy, she finally decided to leave the marriage.

Elle's Story

Elle's husband, Tony, was a plastic surgeon who was beloved by patients and staff alike. He and Elle had four children. He was handsome and charming and had a good reputation in the community, but no one would have guessed the kind of husband he was—controlling and tyrannical.

Elle lived a crazy-making life. Living with Tony was like living with two different people. He could be warm, engaging, and loving one minute, and cold, calculating, and controlling the next. He could turn on a dime, and she never knew which husband she would be dealing with.

When he was good, he was so good that she excused his bad behavior and scolded herself for being overly sensitive. In the good times he was attentive and loving, the ideal husband and devoted father. How could she have doubted him? Elle did everything she could to make the good times last. She accommodated his every whim and exhausted herself trying to please him.

But the bad times came anyway, and they were hell. Tony was insanely jealous and accused Elle of all manner of nonexistent attractions and affairs. He seldom supported her parenting decisions and routinely demeaned her in front of the children. He was intrusive to the point that Elle was not allowed privacy of any kind. He monitored her phone calls and followed her into the bathroom if he wanted to. When her two older boys started treating her like they'd seen their father treat her, she knew she had to leave him—both for herself and for the sake of her children.

"I can't live like this anymore," Elle whimpered the first time I saw her. Tears dropped on her jeans, and her long blond hair fell forward, covering her face. "Lately, the boys are saying the exact same things to me that he says, in exactly the same tone of voice—I can't let this happen! But I'll be breaking up the family. The kids love their dad. Sometimes I think I'm so selfish. I don't know what to do."

We worked together for several months before Elle was ready to take any action. She had the characteristics of a person who suffered from toxic guilt and who had been emotionally abused. She blamed herself for not being a better wife. Why would Tony treat her like that? What had she done wrong?

As time went by, Elle was able to see the truth. She hadn't done anything wrong; her husband was abusive. Elle was healthy enough to believe she deserved more. She knew it was time to claim territory, but she was afraid of what Tony might do: he had money and was charming and powerful. With support from me, her family, and a few good friends, she claimed territory and braced for the storm.

When Elle filed for divorce, Tony pulled out all the stops. He hired the most ruthless lawyer in town and sued for custody of the children. He prolonged litigation and fought her attorney's efforts to secure adequate financial support for Elle and the children during the proceedings. He disparaged her all over town. She was crazy, he told their friends and acquaintances; she had "lost it." He met with the kids' principals, counselors, and teachers, portraying himself as the victim of her unpredictable emotions. He told everyone the rug had been pulled right out from under him, and he had no idea why she was leaving him. He had thought their marriage was secure—she must be having an affair.

The water churned and the waves crashed around her. When parents of her son's soccer teammates snubbed her at a game and gathered around Tony in a blatant show of support, Elle thought she might drown. But with determination and resolve, she reminded herself that she was not bad or deceitful; truth was on her side. With her head held high, she remained afloat.

The legal battle was long and contentious. Although Elle was reassured time and again by her attorney that she would not lose custody of her children, she was terrified nonetheless. As the months dragged by, Elle made use of her support system. She saw me every week and spent time with her friends and family. She got a part-time job. She got stronger, and her self-worth improved.

Before the divorce was finalized, Elle began to realize that it would never be over. Tony would continue to make her life miserable if he could. But as she faced and survived each squall, her confidence grew. She no longer became immobilized when the dark clouds gathered because she could anticipate a storm and calmly take action to protect herself.

Bracing for the Storm When Your Kids Are Ruining Your Life

It is always a matter of *re*-claiming territory if you are the parent and your child or children are trespassing. After all, you were there first. You may have invited them in, but if you do not want them there anymore you have the right to demand they exit the property. Once you have made that clear, expect foul weather.

Bracing for the storm with children is like weatherizing your home for a hurricane. You know the storm is coming, so you make adequate preparations. You can always hope the weather changes for the better and spares you, but it is better to be safe than sorry.

Karen's Story

Karen was an engineer with a thirteen-year-old girl and a nine-year-old boy. I remember sneaking a peek at her through my lobby window as she filled out her intake forms. She had chin-length brown hair, stylish glasses, a single strand of pearls, and a beautifully tailored black suit. I summed her up as controlled and sophisticated. It turned out Karen was anything but controlled and sophisticated. Freaked out and at her wits' end was more like it!

She had been a stay-at-home mom for seven years and had gone back to work two years ago. Her kids did not adjust well to the change; they were used to Mom being at home, catering to their every whim. Karen sheepishly admitted that she liked working outside the home better than in it—it was much easier!

Her youngest was a bright, demanding boy who was a real handful. He delighted in tormenting his sister into rages. Screaming, yelling, and slamming doors was the norm.

Karen traveled for her work and dreaded coming home after a business trip. Compliance with rules for household chores was nonexistent; the house was always a wreck from top to bottom. Complaints and demands greeted her at the door after days of hectic flight schedules, meetings, and deadlines. Both kids whined about the behavior of the other, blaming and tattling.

Karen's husband, Dick, was a mild-mannered man whose parenting style was live-and-let-live. He was at the helm when Karen was away, but he did not really captain the ship. Karen and her husband loved each other and were happy together. However, it was no surprise that the couple squabbled frequently about the messy house and the children's noncompliant behavior—a great example of how kids can ruin the best of marriages.

We went right into couple work. Karen confessed how guilty she felt about going back to work, because it meant she was spending most of her time and energy outside the home. Dick had his own issues with guilt. His father had been demanding and tyrannical, and he swore he would be a different kind of parent. He felt overwhelmingly guilty when he disciplined the kids, so he found it easier to look the other way.

This couple loved each other and decided they had allowed the children too much access to their domain. The crew had mutinied, and it was time to take back the ship. The first step was to institute a system of discipline that both parents could agree upon (similar to ideas outlined in the "Claiming Territory with Children" section of Chapter 16). Re-bonded as teammates and confident of their game plan, they faced the opposition and braced for the storm.

Human beings almost always resist change, and the kids resisted. They used all the guilt-inducing ploys—*You don't love us! I hate you! You're mean! No fair!*—but to no avail. The parents, united in their plan of action, won and reclaimed their territory.

I advise parents to stake out their territory early, build good fences, and maintain them vigilantly. Kids are the wiliest space invaders on the planet.

Safety Measures

It's always good to have a plan when a storm approaches. The following items should be included in your survival kit:

1. **Bedroom door lock.** Install one. Your bedroom should be a safe haven from your children when you need it to be. If your

kids don't really need your attention—if they're not sick or hurt or frightened or in danger—it's fair to claim privacy.

2. **Babysitter.** Find one. All parents need good, reliable babysitters. If you live far away from family (or your family can't or won't babysit for you), search for other sources. Explore your neighborhood; knock on doors if necessary to find out where likely babysitters (teens, young adults, or seniors) live. Call the local high school and speak to a counselor. Contact the student employment center of colleges or universities in the area. Call your church, or a church that is in your neighborhood, and inquire about possible babysitters. Post a notice at your workplace, fitness center, or church, or anywhere in the area that has a bulletin board for public use—libraries and bookstores are good bets. Advertise in local newspapers. Always interview child-care applicants; require references and check them out.

3. **Parents' day out.** Locate a place that provides this service. Nonprofit organizations like churches and community-service leagues may offer low-cost child care on a weekly basis.

4. **Dates.** Have them. Many couples lose each other in the maze of parenting and the demands of work. I work with couples who haven't had a good face-to-face conversation with each other since their last therapy session. No wonder their relationship is in trouble! Ideally, couples should get away on a date once a week—no kids allowed. It doesn't have to be an expensive outing. Trips to a bookstore, evenings at a coffee shop, visits to an art museum, or picnics in the park are great low-cost events where quiet prevails and conversation is possible.

Single parents need dates even more than married people do. Time away from the kids doesn't have to be spent with a romantic interest—women need time with other women, and men need the camaraderie of other men.

5. **Memberships.** Get some. Join a place where child care is provided for members, so you can interact with adults and not have to worry about your children. Fitness centers, churches, and

nonprofit organizations often provide child care for their members when they work out or do volunteer work.

6. **Sex.** Have it. It is not uncommon for parents' sex life to wax, wane, and finally disappear altogether. The loss of the important sexual connection bodes ill for the health of a couple. (The first list item, the bedroom lock, comes in handy here.)

If you're thinking everything mentioned as a safety measure is an escape tactic, you're exactly right! Parents need and deserve adequate non-work-related time away from their children. That is, time away from your children while you are at your job doesn't count. If you love your job and consider it a break from your children, great, but you still need grown-up playtime.

Bracing for the Storm with Disapproving Parents

If you have claimed your territory by doing something your parents do not approve of, there will be consequences. Parental disapproval rips through the souls of approval-seekers. Guilty people want to please their parents, but bracing for the storm means facing their disapproval.

Do not beat yourself up too much if confronting your parents' disapproval has kept you at their beck and call. After all, during the formative years of your life, your very survival depended upon them. And there are cultures that venerate parental approval—one must have it to marry, go into a specific occupation, or attend a certain school. The commandment to honor your parents is well-known in Western culture. It is no wonder that parental approval is so important.

But you have claimed territory and now here you are, facing their condemnation. The first thing to do is remember your adult status. We entered adulthood when we became self-supporting and were no longer subject to our parents' rules. But how fast we regress into childhood when our parents disapprove! You may have children of your own, do a fine job of parenting them, and still find yourself reduced to an adolescent when facing your parents. Remember that you are a grown-up, a fully functioning adult in your own right. You are no longer subordinate to your parent; you are an equal.

Second, ask yourself this question: do I owe my life to my parents because they gave birth to me? The sense of needing to please parents can verge on the feeling that survival is at stake. *If it wasn't for them I wouldn't even be here! I owe them everything!* You owe your parents a lot, but do you really owe them your life?

Finally, although you should never expect unconditional love from anyone because human beings have conditions on their love, you should be able to expect extraordinary love from your parent. The love of a parent for a child is about as close as anyone can come to unconditional love, but some parents are a very long way from loving even slightly unconditionally. Ask yourself what are the conditions your disapproving parents are putting on you. Do your choices have to meet with their approval in order for you to be loved by them? If so, the relationship is not healthy. That certainly does not mean you have to leave the relationship, but knowing this may help you brace for the storm with added resolve.

Marty's story illustrates the power of parent-pleasing and the struggle to breaking free.

Marty's Story

It was Marty's first appointment. Her intake form indicated she was twenty-six, a physical therapist, and newly divorced. A petite brunette, she wore green print hospital scrubs. Flopping on my sofa like she was at the home of an old friend, she reached for a tissue, put her gum in it, and said, "You've got to help me—I'm screwing everyone in town!"

She had been dating like crazy ever since her divorce seven months ago. She was drinking too much, smoking a fair amount of pot, and hanging out at bars and clubs more nights than not. If she met a man she liked, she was apt to go home with him.

"The worst part is—I'm loving it!" She smiled mischievously.

When she could see that I was not interested in lecturing her about the dangerous emotional and physical consequences of her behavior, she signed on for some intense work.

After several weeks of focusing on her chaotic relationships with men, the heart of her story came out. Marty had been sexually abused by her stepfather. She never called it abuse because he had never had intercourse with her, but he had fondled her several times and sexualized their relationship in other ways. When she was a teenager he insisted that she sit on his lap, rub his back, and lie with him on the sofa to watch television. If she begged off or refused, he punished her by withdrawing; sometimes he would not speak to her for days. She had no privacy; he found reasons to come into the bathroom when she was showering and would wander into her bedroom when she was in her underwear. She reported these things to her mother, who either minimized the significance of the problem or blamed Marty for being suggestive.

I explained that such behavior was indeed sexual abuse. Her personal space, boundaries, and privacy had been invaded. Her mother's response was tragically irresponsible.

Marty's biological father was an alcoholic, and her mother had left him when Marty was an infant. He had made no attempt to be involved in Marty's life; in fact, she had never seen him. Thus, the most important men in her life had either abandoned her or abused her. The seeds of her sexual promiscuity were sown in those failed relationships.

Marty and her mother were quite close. They were both single women (her mother and stepfather had eventually divorced). They called each other every day, got together for meals and movies, and took trips together on occasion. Marty told me that she had tried to talk with her mother about her ex-stepfather's abuse, but her mother refused to discuss it. If Marty brought the subject up, her mother became upset and distanced herself. Marty couldn't tolerate the rupture in their relationship, so she quit trying to talk about the past.

Her mother's approval was very important to Marty; she was the only parent Marty had. But over time, Marty was able to identify the sense of betrayal she felt, as well as the anger she held deep inside, because when she was a vulnerable child her mother had neither protected her nor believed her.

Although Marty's mother had made it clear that talking about the past was "off-limits," Marty decided that in order for her to heal she had to claim territory and have the conversation. Bracing for the storm, in this case, meant preparing for her mother's reaction when she confronted her about the most sensitive subject between them.

She suspected her mother blamed herself, and she had no way to know if her mother could tolerate the confrontation. Even though Marty knew that her mother might leave their relationship, she knew she had to do it. The stakes were high, but Marty was not alone. She had me, her therapist, and her best girlfriend to support her.

The confrontation was more like a tornado than a storm. There were accusations and denial. Marty's mother could not or would not accept responsibility for her part in the abuse. Finally, Marty's mother ran crying from the house.

Marty had to sort out her past in order to go forward in life with a better sense of self. Unfortunately, she and her mother fell out of their relationship in the process.

There is a happy ending to this story. Marty maintained her position but continued to be in contact with her mother via e-mail. When she became engaged and was planning a wedding, her mother made a tearful phone call, apologizing and asking for forgiveness. Mother and daughter are in a relationship today.

Although staying in a relationship with a parent is the best option, it is not always possible. Sometimes, losing a relationship with a parent may be necessary when you are escaping toxic guilt. Such was the case in Jackie's story.

Jackie's Story

Jackie's childhood was traumatic and chaotic because her mother was an alcoholic. There were multiple boyfriends and multiple moves. It was commonplace for Jackie to stumble upon a strange man in her mother's bedroom or to come home from school to find her belongings packed in a U-Haul. Her mother's life was a series of losses—men, jobs, and friends. Jackie finally escaped from the madness by going to live with her aunt.

As the years went by, she tried and tried again to have some semblance of a normal relationship with her mother, but to no avail. The craziness was always there, and there was always another drunken episode. But Jackie continued to believe it was her responsibility to make a relationship with her mother work.

She graduated from high school and went on to college, clinging to the hope that things with her mother would be different. She hoped, prayed, phoned often, wrote, and visited. Nothing changed. Over and over, with renewed optimism and rekindled expectation, Jackie tried to establish a healthy mother-daughter relationship.

Jackie accommodated her mother's every whim in an attempt to make it all better, but every encounter ended in disappointment. Emotionally exhausted and racked with guilt, Jackie entered therapy. What was she doing wrong?

Jackie had no clue that she had a right to her own territory. She did not realize she could choose a healthy, emotionally safe existence for herself. But at this point in her life, Jackie did know that her mother was not emotionally safe for her. Jackie kept returning to the center of the ring, only to get beat up again and again. It was time for new rules.

In the course of therapy, Jackie learned how to protect herself from her mother. She wrote her mother a heartfelt letter expressing her love and telling her mother what it would take for her to be able to stay in a relationship with her. Her mother had to be sober when they talked on the phone. Her mother had to be sober when Jackie visited. She could no longer discuss the details of her latest romance with her daughter.

By writing that letter, Jackie had effectively claimed her territory. Now, however, it was time to brace for the storm. The storm was not her mother's anger, it was her mother's disregard.

Although her mother promised to comply with her daughter's demands, nothing changed. Her mother continued in her old patterns, expecting Jackie to take care of her and let her off the hook when she misbehaved. So Jackie gently but firmly withdrew from the relationship. She stopped calling her mother and stopped accepting calls from her. Eventually, she got a new cell phone so her mother couldn't harass her with repeated calls anymore. She returned mail from her mother unopened. It was a difficult transition, but one that spelled freedom and increased health for Jackie.

Encountering a storm is a real tribulation if you still need financial support from your parents. We will always want and need emotional support and affection from our parents, but adults don't depend upon their parents for financial support. I have seen many a suffering person stuck tight in their parents' grip because going against their wishes would mean financial loss. If you need your parents to pay tuition, make your rent or house payment, finance your car, or pay your insurance, you are not ready to claim your territory with them. Nor are you ready if you are depending on an inheritance from them.

Storm Shelters

When it is obvious that a storm is approaching, it is only prudent to head for shelter. Just think of the scene from *The Wizard of Oz* when everyone except Dorothy dashes to the storm shelter as the tornado approaches. Family and farmhands huddled together in safety while Dorothy returned to the house. I recall the thoughts and feelings the scene evoked in me as a child. As the little community of friends pulled the storm door closed behind them I felt relief—they were together and would be OK. At the same time I felt my stomach roll with fear and dread as Dorothy, alone, went back into the house.

So it will be when you decide to claim territory—the storm will come. You need to know where to go for shelter when it does. You will find comfort in the presence of select others and fear if you go it alone. The following section will help you identify ways to protect yourself so, when it is time, you can gather your resources and wait for the storm to pass feeling as safe and protected as possible.

Bracing for the Storm by Connecting to God

One of the most powerful things you can do when contemplating an action that will have unpleasant consequences is to spend some time getting as spiritually connected as possible. When you feel the presence of God, it is amazing what you can do. This connection doesn't always come naturally or easily, however. I recommend getting all the help you can.

Figure out what you can do to embrace your spiritual connection. My husband finds his best connection to God in nature. When he's frazzled and at odds with himself and his life, he goes fishing. He tells me that standing waist-deep in a trout stream, in silence and solitude, he can remember who he is and whose he is.

I have knee-buckling gratitude for the institutional church. I need a community of believers around me. I need to worship, read, meet in groups, spend one-on-one time with spiritual advisors, and volunteer at church. I also make at least two retreats a year.

If you've never made a retreat, you owe it to yourself; and if you're bracing for the storm, it could be crucial. There are retreat centers all over the country. These places of silence, solitude, and hospitality offer lodging and meals for people seeking a time-out from their lives to nurture their relationship with God. You can count on accommodations that are comfortable and food that is nourishing—simplicity is the norm. Usually the monks or nuns or community residents observe a schedule of daily worship, and it is customary that retreat guests are invited to join them.

You can turn any time away from your usual life into a spiritual retreat. Go somewhere by yourself or stay at home alone. The *intention* of your retreat is what counts. Devote your time to prayer, reflection, reading, writing or journaling, and resting. Invite God to be your constant companion. Retreats can fuel your spiritual tank for the journey of claiming territory and bracing for the storm.

Bracing for the Storm with the Help of Others

I do not want to underestimate the difficulty of Step Three. Preparing yourself to be whipped about by an emotional gale-force storm goes against our sense of self-preservation. What most of us want is peace and harmony. In the face of such a storm we would rather run for cover, try to save face, or find a way to avoid controversy.

There do not seem to be many highly visible figures—politicians, pastors, athletes, or stars—who are able to face a storm head-on when confronted with a situation in which they would lose approval. But to escape toxic guilt, it is a must—and that means that you or I, ordinary folks, are called to a challenge many famous people cannot meet.

Enlist the help of others when storm reports are out. A support team is your best bet, but if a one-person support system is all you can muster, be grateful that you have an advocate. Choose that person carefully, however. Do not seek support from someone you know does not see things your way. You would never believe how many people will turn for support to the last person on the planet who would understand and be helpful or truly supportive.

If your mother does not approve of what you'd like to do—move in with your boyfriend, quit a job you despise, or send your kids to day care—do not go to her for support. If your religious tradition is opposed to abortion, divorce, or homosexuality, do not go to your minister if you have one of these issues. Do not confide in your best friend if you know he or she could not support your decision to go back to work, move, finish that college degree, or go on a singles cruise.

Find someone you respect who will encourage you on your path. Spend time with that person, study that person, and if you wish you were more like that person, start acting like him or her. Such a person could be a friend, a coach, a relative, a pastor, a therapist, or a colleague.

Enlisting a community of supporters is helpful to many people who have claimed their territory and are bracing for the storm. When I left my marriage, I was not prepared for the social and cultural storm that followed. I moved into a nice, quiet suburban neighborhood as a single mom with three teenagers. No one knocked on the door to welcome us to the block. Two years later, I still hadn't met a neighbor.

Then the house we had been renting was sold to a couple. On the day they moved in, I went over to be sure everything was in order. When I got there, the new owners were being greeted by a cluster of neighbors bearing cakes and cookies—a welcoming committee of sorts. It finally dawned on me that a single mother and her children were not an acceptable family model for that neighborhood.

Shortly after my divorce, I was visiting with a friend after church during the coffee hour. "Let me give you some advice," she said, lowering her voice. "Don't talk to anyone's husband too long." At first I did not even know what she meant—but then I got it. I was a threat. Wives would be threatened by my single status. Would I be interested in their husband? And husbands did not want their wives in the company of a woman who was enjoying being single. Would I give them ideas?

As a divorcée, my status had changed, and I was not prepared for it. Facing the storm meant recognizing that I was a single woman navigating the waters of polite society in a medium-sized community in the Midwest—not the easiest position to be in. The best thing I ever did was to organize a group of other single women. We understood each other. We went out to dinner and got together in each other's homes, where there was great conversation and lots of laughter. We provided emotional support to each other, and we all grew stronger.

Most communities offer divorce support groups so one does not have to endure the divorce process alone. Singles groups are also widely available and may offer a variety of activities like volleyball leagues, dinner clubs, book clubs, and bridge groups. You may find such groups in churches, mental health agencies, or in the offices of private practitioners.

I've offered such groups myself through the years. One of my groups organized a closing event to follow the last session. When the meeting ended, a limo appeared. The group piled in and went to a local club for drinks, and later they had a "Divorce House Tour." They drove by all the houses they had acquired or lost in their divorces. All reports were that it was a hilarious and fun-filled evening.

Another time to call on others is when you have reclaimed territory from a child. You can count on facing a storm every time there are new requests from your child and you hold the line. Your child will expect you to cave in when he or she wants to move back home, or calls you from juvenile detention and promises to return to school, or promises to get back on track if you'll just make a loan of $500, co-sign for a car, or help finance this great get-rich-quick scheme. When you say no, the wind will howl and the storm will rage (or the silence will be deafening, which can be worse).

At times like these, it is good to have a support network lined up so you are not trying to maintain your boundaries alone. Tough Love groups have been helpful to many parents standing their ground for their own sake and the sake of their child. Check your local newspaper or phone book or go to www.toughlove.org.

Escaping toxic guilt is an active process, and you must be intentional about following each step. In Step Three, you prepare for the difficult experience of enduring other people's displeasure, disapproval, or downright wrath because of what you have decided to do. Find spiritual and emotional support so that you do not have to walk through the storm alone; then you are ready for Step Four, Ride the Wind.

18

Step Four:
Ride the Wind

As you work your way through the first three steps of escaping toxic guilt, you learn to become proactive in your own behalf and take control of your life. In Step One, you speak the truth by confessing the reality of your situation first to yourself and then to someone else. In Step Two, you claim territory by taking control of your personal emotional space. And in Step Three, you brace for the storm by preparing for the disapproval of others and standing your ground. Step Four is different. When it is time for Step Four, it is time to let go, relinquish control, and accept the results.

Letting Go and Finding Freedom

Learning to take control is an important part of overcoming toxic guilt, but learning to let go of control is equally important. In fact, letting go is so important that the older I get, the more I think that life is all about letting go.

I have a picture in my office from StoryPeople.com, the website of Brian Andreas, artist and storyteller. One of the whimsical, bright-colored characters is hanging on to a pole like a flag. The picture says:

> If you hold on to the
> handle, she said,

> it's easier to maintain
> the illusion of control.
> But it's more fun
> if you just let the wind
> carry you.

I love the promise of freedom this verse implies. However, letting go is much more difficult than it seems, and it is especially challenging for people who live with toxic guilt. That is because guilty people are the responsible ones; they love approval and they like to get things right. They need to think of themselves as being good, doing the right thing, and being liked by others. "Work ethic" is their middle name.

The guilt-ridden accept the adage "God helps those who help themselves" as truth. Plenty of them think it's straight out of the Bible (it isn't).

Letting go is counterintuitive to guilty people, but it's a skill that must be learned and practiced in order to recover from toxic guilt. Guilty people are usually responsible people—and sometimes, responsible people have a high need for control.

If you have a high need for control, I bet you know it on some level. There are a couple of important things to consider when you explore your need for control. One is a psychological issue; the other is a cultural/religious issue.

Letting Go as a Psychological Issue

I discussed the effect of parental neglect on the developing self in Chapter 5 when I explored how pseudo-victims are made. Here, I will show you how the same circumstance, parental neglect, can lead to a high need for control.

In the course of their natural development, human beings are dependent upon others for a long time. Infants and young children are dependent upon others (usually their parents) for survival. As we get older we need family members, teachers, coaches, ministers, and ultimately close friends, lovers, or spouses to meet our need for physical protection and emotional development. We learn to trust others as others meet our needs. Unfortunately, not everyone gets their needs met adequately.

If, somewhere along the way, those who were supposed to protect you and meet your needs failed in these tasks and you were injured, your ability to trust others is compromised. You may become protective, defensive, guarded, and self-absorbed, and believe that you had better take care of yourself because you doubt that anyone else will. You may not be able to feel safe unless you are in control of situations, events, and people.

These psychological positions wreak havoc in intimate relationships, where a balance between dependence on yourself and dependence on another person is crucial. Both people in a relationship need to feel a sense of power, and if one person is intent on being in charge, the result will be conflict, disappointment, and ultimately, rejection. Also, a high need for control in all aspects of one's life is a blueprint for emotional angst because in the human condition we are really in control of so little.

If you have a high need for control, you are bound to have good reasons for it. Maybe in childhood, adolescence, or even adulthood you were betrayed, disappointed, wounded, or endangered because someone close to you let you down. Trusting another to keep you safe turned out to be a bad mistake.

Pain is a masterful teacher; therefore, you vowed to keep the reins in your own hands from then on. Although this is usually not a conscious decision, somewhere deep inside you came to believe that if you are in control, you can keep from being hurt again. The need to be in control is fear-based, and letting go can threaten your sense of security. If you let go, it may feel like opening the door to chaos, destruction, and failure—no wonder you hang on for dear life!

Learning to let go will feel strange, even frightening, but learn you must. Remember how you felt when you learned to do something new such as jump off the diving board, ride a bike, or venture onto the ice with skates? You were afraid, but you did it anyway. That principle also applies to letting go. Allow yourself to feel the fear, and then do what you need to do anyway.

Letting Go as a Cultural/Religious Issue

Letting go is an idea that is countercultural to people in the West. The importance of taking charge, stepping up to the plate, charting your own course, and being the master of your destiny are the cultural messages that we grow up with. Power, dominance, and control are the ideals in Western culture. Letting go implies weakness, surrender, and failure, so the very words *letting go* are suspect. However, letting go is truly wisdom in many situations, and letting go of what other people think of you is a step toward freedom for people with toxic guilt. So is letting go of the compulsion to rush in and rescue everyone in your path.

Letting go is a religious issue as well. If you believe in an all-powerful and compassionate God, it may be easier to let go and trust the outcome of events. Perhaps you can trust that God will be the wind beneath your wings and keep you airborne. But many people who profess faith in a compassionate divine being find they cannot let go and trust the invisible Force when push comes to shove. Instead, they fight to take charge of circumstances beyond their control. The result is usually fear and frustration.

To overcome what seems for some people to be an inherent distrust of letting go, I suggest you practice letting go in the small things. Say a little prayer, something like "OK God, I'm putting this in your hands," and do your best to let go of a small concern. See what happens. Your ability to trust that God is not only in charge, but actually cares about you, may improve if you can manage to get out of the way so that God can act. If you do not believe in God, or you are not so sure about that all-powerful and compassionate part, you have a tough question to answer: *if I'm not in control, who is?*

Learning to let go paves the way to freedom for people with a proclivity toward rescuing others. The operative word is *learning.* Letting go won't come naturally or easily for you if your lifelong practice has been to weigh in and take charge. That is what rescuers do.

If you are a rescuer, I am not suggesting you stop helping those in need, but I am suggesting that you curb your inclination to aid and assist everyone who crosses your path. I encourage you to use discrimination about how, when, where, and who you attempt to rescue.

I was talking to a colleague not long ago about this very thing. She is a burned-out caregiver who is a rescuer in both her public and her personal life. Angela took on the needs of all comers; letting go was not in her vocabulary.

Angela's Story

Angela is a therapist, and everyone she knows turns to her for help—family, friends, and clients. Her family is chaotic and needy, and her client population is among the most challenging. Most of her clients are court-ordered to enter therapy. Treating adolescent substance abusers and high-conflict families of divorce is the order of the day for Angela.

Not long ago she told me she was resigning from her position at a community mental health center. She said, "I can't carry emotionally crippled people anymore—I'm too tired."

I was saddened, because Angela is one of the best clinicians I know. Her work is beyond reproach. She has the rare gift of genuine compassion seamlessly balanced with therapeutic confrontation. Her resignation will be a loss to the community. If her rescuing had been more balanced—if she had learned to let go a little and not try to save the world alone, she probably would not be leaving her career.

Rescuers often resign like that, in an exhausted heap and all too soon. For rescuers, letting go may mean stepping *back* rather than stepping in. If you are a rescuer, for the sake of saving yourself you must learn to step back from responding indiscriminately to the emotional needs of others.

Dr. Bradshaw's Story

I have a story on that theme from my graduate-school days. Dr. Bradshaw was one of my favorite professors. He looked like Freud, but he acted more like Yoda. He had a ring of white hair and a neatly cropped beard of the same color. His gentle and often mischievous eyes peered out from little round glasses. He was very wise. He had been a student of Carl Rogers—a famous name in the counseling profession—and he carried the torch passed on to him by the master with a certain light grace. He supported, challenged, and intrigued his students. We loved him. He was also an excellent therapist.

One day, Dr. Bradshaw began his class with a question. "What is the first rule of therapy?" he asked us, folding his arms and leaning against the chalkboard in his characteristically casual way. Tentatively, a few hands went up.

"Is it to always have positive regard for the client?" posed the eager student.

"No," was the reply.

"That you should never impose your agenda on the client?" another classmate offered.

"Nope."

"You should have a number of models for doing therapy to draw from and not depend upon just one?" another ventured.

"No."

"Could it be that your empathic skills, the ability to really 'be with' your client, is the most important thing?" a frowning future therapist suggested.

"No."

Several more attempts were made, but each was dismissed with the now-predictable rejection. We were beginning to become uneasy and shift around in our seats. We looked at one another, searching for a sign that one of us had the correct answer, but we could only roll our eyes and shrug our shoulders to acknowledge defeat. Finally, we threw in the towel.

"The first rule of therapy," the wily professor stated as we all leaned forward in expectation, "is that the therapist must survive."

I have found that adage to be one of the most important things I learned in graduate school. It is absolutely true and particularly useful for those in the helping professions. Nurses, doctors, therapists, teachers, ministers, and others who devote their careers to service have a high rate of burnout. But they are not the only ones; accountants, lawyers, mothers, fathers, sisters, construction workers, and cab drivers may also be at risk.

If toxic guilt keeps you jumping to the ready every time someone seems to need you, then you are also at risk for burnout. The next time you position yourself at the starting gate for yet another rescue, I invite you to try something new. Catch yourself and stop. Then ask yourself this question: *can I step into this situation and still maintain my emotional balance?* If the answer is no, step back. When guilt washes through you like a wave because you are not responding in your old knee-jerk way, tell yourself that in order to survive, you must learn how to let go.

Letting Go of Approval and Finding Freedom

I have seen far too many good people allow the needs and approval of others to determine the outcome of their lives. They carefully chart a course through the stars but abort the mission the minute they encounter someone else's troubles. It is one thing to be sensitive to the wishes of others; it is another to allow the wishes of others to consistently ride roughshod over your plans.

My Story

When I began my stint as a college chaplain, I worked at a facility with several other campus ministers. One of them had a lot of experience and was very welcoming and helpful. He even invited me to partner with him in running our ministries together. At first I was delighted with the plan and our relationship flourished.

But over time, as I found my place and found my voice, our relationship changed. My colleague was not comfortable sharing leadership of our ministries, and there was no room for my input and ideas. I tried to be a diplomat, but I was not willing to be a doormat. How could I maintain our relationship and the positive feelings I once had about my colleague and still claim my territory? I tried everything I could think of to ease the tension between us, but the storm continued to gather force. At my wits' end, I sought the counsel of my superior and spoke the truth (Step One). He encouraged me to stay the course.

Finally, push came to shove when I disagreed with the other minister about a major project. There did not seem to be room for compromise, so I claimed territory (Step Two) and held my ground. Then I gathered my support system around me and braced for the storm (Step Three). When it came, it was a tempest. I knew my colleague did not approve of me, and now I knew for a fact that he did not like me either.

That was rough enough, but when he lobbied for my overthrow I had to tie myself to the mast. I knew in my head that I was doing the right thing, but my gut heaved and rolled. I was in uncharted waters; this was *way* out of character for me. I was making a fuss and bucking the system—bad, bad girl! After all, my usual style was inviting others to have a lovely ride on my boat, not throw them overboard!

Slowly but surely I let go of my need for his (and others') approval and rode the wind (Step Four). When I did, an amazing transformation began to unfold; the worry and tension I carried like a heavy backpack slipped off. It simply did not matter anymore that my colleague not only did not approve of me but also did not like me one bit. I was cordial and polite but continued to hold my ground.

His attitude did not change; but even though I experienced his disdain on a daily basis, I felt lighter, freer, and more myself than I had for a long time. Now, as I think back on that episode in my life I smile with gratitude. Learning to let go brought freedom and a guilt-free sense of self.

Myra and Chris's Story

Myra and Chris had been married eleven years and had a seven-year-old daughter. After two years of marriage they had separated for several months but were able to put the relationship back together. However, the issues that precipitated the separation were never resolved. Conflict simmered and boil-overs were common. Unable to resolve their differences themselves, they decided to try couples coaching.

Myra complained that she felt like a single mother because Chris did almost nothing to help her run the household or care for their child. Indignant and defensive, Chris claimed his hard work outside the home was not appreciated—and that moreover, Myra was distant, cold, and unaffectionate.

When Myra and I met in an individual session, she told me that she wanted out of the marriage, and had for some time, but felt too guilty to take action. Nothing had changed since their brief separation eight years ago. She had had it with Chris's refusal to help her, was fed up with his quick temper, and sick of his preoccupation with his real love, bicycle racing.

The trouble was that she worried about him; how could he manage without her? She worried about her daughter; how would divorce impact the child's life? And she worried about her parents' reaction. Myra was from a religious family who didn't believe in divorce. She could not bear to think about how upset her parents would be if she left the marriage.

When she spoke the truth (Step One), I was able to help her. We worked on claiming territory (Step Two), and over time she came to believe that her happiness was as important as Chris's. She decided that it was not her responsibility to take care of Chris's adjustment to becoming single. It became clear to her that as long as her child was safe and loved, she was fulfilling her job as a mother. She also learned that being from a broken home could be less damaging to a child than being in an intact family where marital conflict was the order of the day. Finally, she was able to understand that as an adult, she was not obligated to please her parents in every major life decision she made.

Eventually, Myra braced for the storm (Step Three) and filed for divorce. Chris did his best to make her life miserable. He besmirched her name all over town, withheld money, stalked her, and told their daughter that it was all Mommy's fault that they were divorcing. Her parents' response was equally negative. They were critical, judgmental, cold, and distant.

Riding the Wind (Step Four) was difficult for Myra. A voice inside her was saying, *Chris is right! It is all my fault. Maybe I overreacted; maybe my life wasn't so bad—I'm asking for too much.* However, Chris's aggressive, controlling behavior reassured her that she'd done the right thing for herself. And although her parents' reaction was painful, Myra discovered she had other important people in her life who understood and supported her.

In order to let go of worrying about how her decision would affect others, Myra had to choose to see things differently. Her knee-jerk perspective was to blame herself and feel guilty for causing others distress. But this time she was intentional about steering away from the old thinking. She took care of herself by continuing individual therapy and calling on a couple of girlfriends who understood what she had been going through. She was careful to nurture her spiritual resources, too. Feeling good about herself, close to God, and strong in her resolve to forge a new life, she was able to let go of the guilt she felt about ending her marriage and move on.

Finding Freedom Through Forgiveness

Forgiveness is a key to riding the wind. If you can learn to forgive others for the storm they send your way when you claim your territory, it is much easier to let go of their critical, judgmental responses. Learning to forgive others enables you to forgive yourself, which is the most difficult process for guilty folks!

Jesus Christ was a huge proponent of forgiveness. He commanded his followers to forgive others and made it clear that a forgiving nature was pleasing to God. But He did not tell his disciples how to forgive. Thanks to research in the field of psychology, we now have some good ideas about how to think about forgiveness and how to enter into the process.

Forgiveness was not a topic for exploration when I was in graduate school. The study of forgiveness was considered religious in nature, something that belonged in seminary curriculums. The work of forgiveness fell to clergy.

Happily, things have changed. Scholars of psychology began researching the emotional consequences of forgiveness, and study after study documented that forgiveness brought emotional healing to those who practiced it. On the other hand, a lack of forgiveness left people in varying degrees of dis-ease. Once again, psychology had caught up with religion. Now forgiveness is studied in the field of psychology as an important component of emotional health.

Although there is a lot of misunderstanding about forgiveness, a comprehensive discussion of it is beyond the scope of this book. There are excellent books available on the topic. Mental health professionals and others propose models of forgiveness that are compassionate, make sense, and promote healing. I hope that the following principles, like beams from a lighthouse, are enough to help you steer in the right direction:

- To forgive does not mean to forget. The Bible assures us that when God forgives, God forgets; but human beings do not.
- To forgive does not mean to excuse bad behavior. You can forgive someone and still hold them accountable for their bad behavior. For example, you might forgive a business partner who cheated you but still litigate against him.
- Empathy is crucial in forgiveness. Try to put yourself in the other person's place; see the situation from his or her perspective. (This is incredibly challenging, but worth the effort!)
- If you are having trouble forgiving someone, recall times when you were forgiven by others.
- When you do not forgive, you are bound to the person who wronged you. Forgiveness is about your freedom. (Note: it won't work if you forgive only to gain your own freedom. You must have compassion for the person you are forgiving.)
- Forgiveness does not mean you will accept the person's bad behavior in the future.
- Forgiving another does not mean you must welcome that person back into your life. Reconciliation, a separate process, is the act of reuniting with another.

- The person who offended you does not have to ask for forgiveness. It is a gift freely given, often to the unrepentant and undeserving.
- The person who offended you does not have to know you have forgiven him or her.
- Forgiveness is a process, not a single event.
- Pick a moment in time to pinpoint your decision to forgive. Write a note to yourself documenting your decision, or tell someone about it. Recall your decision to forgive when anger and resentment raise their ugly heads.
- Let go of the notion that things will be different in the future with the person you have forgiven. In other words, have no expectation that the person will change.
- You do not have to forgive the person's bad behavior; you forgive the person for not being able to manage his or her life better.

Practice makes perfect. The more diligent you are in forgiving, the better you'll get at it. Over time, an attitude of forgiveness will grow in you. As a forgiving spirit develops, you will be able to begin forgiving yourself.

Shawna and Tyrone's Story

Shawna and Tyrone looked like the perfect couple. Married five years, they had a bouncing baby boy. Shawna was a stay-at-home mom and Tyrone was a financial planner. They had a new home in the suburbs, a community of friends, and close ties to their parents. Yet here they sat, fidgeting nervously on my sofa. "Shawna doesn't think she loves me anymore," Tyrone said softly, looking at her intently as he spoke. Shawna, painfully thin with dark circles under her eyes, avoided making eye contact with him.

I learned in the course of working with this couple that Tyrone was right; Shawna didn't love him anymore. In individual sessions,

Shawna explained that Tyrone was a good person, a loving husband, and a wonderful father. He had a stellar work ethic and was beloved by friends and family. However, she felt nothing for him. There was no chemistry and no passion. The tear-the-wallpaper-off-the-wall kind of sexual desire she had experienced with other men had never been there for her with Tyrone. At age thirty-two, she decided she didn't want to live without that for the rest of her life.

Shawna berated herself for her inability to love her husband as she wanted. He was a perfectly good human being. She tried in vain to make herself feel something she could not feel. Too guilt-ridden to tell anyone, Shawna kept her secret, but over time her guilty feelings took their toll and she became ill. She lost weight, became clinically depressed, and hated herself. All the joy had left her life.

At last, Shawna spoke the truth (Step One) and shared her feelings with her mother, then with her best friend, and finally with Tyrone. After the truth came out, the couple did not know what to do and sought professional help.

In our first couples session Tyrone made no bones about his goal; he wanted his wife back. Shawna was vague and unable or unwilling to articulate her wishes or goals for therapy. The next week I saw her in an individual session. She told me then that her goal for doing couples work was to find a way to leave the marriage.

Although wracked with guilt, Shawna had healthy ego strength. She did not want to continue to live a lie. The concept of Step Two, claiming territory, made perfect sense to her. We talked about defining boundaries, and when she applied the idea to her life she knew what she had to do. With compassion but resolve she told Tyrone there was no way for her to feel something she did not feel, and that she was not willing to continue in a marital relationship without those feelings. She stood firm and maintained her position against his disbelief and insistence that they could make it work.

For Shawna, bracing for the storm (Step Three) meant facing her friends and extended family as the bad one, the crazy bitch. "Have you lost your mind?" one of her best girlfriends gasped in dismay when Shawna explained she was getting out of her marriage. No one understood. Shawna maintained her resolve and went on as best she could. Riding the wind (Step Four) and letting go of her need for approval from others was hard, but Shawna had learned that staying in the wrong marriage because everyone else approved of the union was not a healthy choice. Slowly but surely, as she took each step down the path to freedom, Shawna was able to forgive her judgmental family and friends. Finally, she forgave herself for not loving her husband.

Letting Go Through Acceptance

Acceptance is another key to letting go. If you can learn to willingly receive whatever flows through your life, you can learn to let it go as well.

When my husband and I make our annual fall trek to the mountains of Colorado, we inevitably spend an hour or two perched on some smooth boulder at the edge of a bubbling stream. I watch the gold-speckled aspen leaves caught in the current as the river carries them down the mountain. The river rocks that stick up just above the water's surface create churning whirlpools where the leaves spin and twist. Sometimes they channel the frothy golden brew into quiet bowls where the leaves lie quietly, awaiting release.

The rocks, impervious to the comings and goings of the leaves, peacefully hold their place. Would that we could cultivate such repose. Instead, we struggle and thrash about, reaching frantically for what we desire and greedily clinging to it, or running from what we fear and disdainfully pushing away what we do not want. This is not acceptance. Nor is acceptance a throwing up of hands in defeat. Acceptance does not mean one tolerates the intolerable without resistance. The acceptance I am talking about is the kind that comes after people in your life do not respond as you would like them to when you claim your territory and hold your ground.

It could be that your spouse decides to leave you because you are no longer willing to sacrifice yourself to meet his or her needs anymore, or some of your family members cut you off because you come out to them or terminate a pregnancy, or your teen-age daughter refuses to speak to you because you have decided to move, or your mother-in-law boycotts Thanksgiving because you won't do it her way this year. These are painful consequences of refusing to allow guilt to control your life, but with acceptance you can let go of them and ride the wind.

This kind of acceptance can be summed up in three words: *what is, is*. Acceptance means that you stop hanging on to things as they were or as you wish they would be. Things are what they are.

The Man on Crete's Story

My favorite story about acceptance and letting go was told in a sermon by one of my favorite pastors. I learned later that she heard the story in a narrative theology course in seminary. The tale brings hope to and inspires courage in those who want to learn to let go.

Once there was a man who lived on the island of Crete. He loved the island as he loved nothing else. At a very old age, and on his deathbed, the man begged to be taken from his bed and placed on the ground of his beloved island. His request was honored, and just before taking his last breath the old man grasped some dirt, clutched it lovingly in his hand, and died.

Suddenly he stood outside Heaven's gates. Saint Peter approached and said, "You have been a good and worthy person. Come, join me in heaven."

The old man moved to follow Saint Peter. "Wait a minute," said Saint Peter, noticing the old man's hand. "You'll have to drop that handful of dirt first. No one may enter heaven with anything but himself."

"Never!" the old man cried in earnest. "I'll never let go of the dirt from my precious island!"

"As you wish," said the gentle saint, and he walked through the great gate, leaving the old man behind.

Years passed, and then one day a beautiful female angel appeared at the gate in a blue and white garment that shone like the moon. Smiling with compassion, she spread her arms. "Come and join us in the Kingdom of Heaven. We've been waiting and waiting."

The old man struggled to right his bent body and lifted his bony fist. "Never! I'll never let go of the earth from my beautiful island!"

The good lady's arms dropped to her side, and melancholy clouded her face. "As you wish," she said sadly, and glided back through Heaven's gates.

Many more years passed, and the old man continued to wait outside the gates. One bright day, the gate swung open and his little great-great-granddaughter came running out. Her red pigtails bounced and her face was aglow. "Grandfather!" She stretched out her hand to him. "Please come with me! We're all waiting for you!"

The old man was so moved by the sight of the child that he instinctively reached for her hand. When he did so, the dirt he'd been holding for so long sifted through his fingers. Hand-in-hand they walked through the gate. And there, just on the other side, was his blessed island of Crete.

Letting go may mean finding the thing that you have always wanted, and for people escaping toxic guilt, freedom is the prize.

19

Step Five:
Patrol Borders

Step Five, the last step, comes after you have learned to change your behavior in order to live life on your own terms. If it is your nature to be sensitive about and responsive to the needs of others, which is a gift to cherish and share, it is important to understand that it is also a gift that you need to protect. Your ability to take care of others must be balanced with the ability to take care of yourself.

When much of your life has been lived on other people's terms and you have finally chosen to change that, you must be careful not to backslide. Step Five will teach you how to nurture and protect your new sense of self.

The Crying Game

Do not underestimate the power of doing what comes naturally, of how strong the temptation to fall back into old habits can be. Over time, the lure of the familiar can pull you back into old patterns. A story told in the film *The Crying Game* illustrates the power of doing what comes naturally:

A scorpion needed to get across a swollen river. The current was swift, and the scorpion was afraid. A frog happened by.

"I must get across the river, and I don't swim. Oh please, Mr. Frog, carry me across the river!" pleaded the scorpion.

"No!" replied the frog. "You're a scorpion, and you'll sting me to death!"

"I won't, I won't! I promise," vowed the scorpion. "I'll be too grateful that you got me across."

The frog reconsidered. "Well, all right, but be careful. Here, climb on my back."

The frog swam the scorpion through the rough water, struggling with his burden. Upon reaching the bank, the scorpion stung the frog to death.

The moral of the story is that the ending should not be a surprise. Both creatures behaved appropriately. It is the nature of a frog to swim and the nature of a scorpion to sting.

Knowing Your Nature

If it is your nature or habit to let guilt keep you from doing what you want to do, you must engage your mind to override your instincts. You have to be very intentional about freeing yourself from the toxic guilt that enslaved you and kept you from doing what you wanted and needed to do. This is not easy; it takes diligence and perseverance.

To patrol your borders is to be on the lookout for old behavior. When you find yourself moving to the starting gate for yet another rescue, try something new. Catch yourself and stop. Ask yourself this question: *can I step into this situation and maintain my emotional balance?* This question may keep you from jumping into the deep end without a life jacket, and the answer may help you curtail your automatic tendency to take on too much.

The answer may even help you see that you should take no action at all. When guilt washes through you like a wave because you are not responding in your old unthinking way, remind yourself of the "Survival Rule" from the last chapter: no matter what happens, I must survive.

Rediscover the Real You

As mentioned in Chapter 9, many people with toxic guilt lose their identity in a relationship, a career, or a role (such as mother, father, daughter, son, doctor, contractor, teacher, and so on). Over time, their sense of self disappears as they automatically respond to what other people want and expect from them.

If this has happened to you, you have the opportunity to rediscover, or discover for the first time, the real you. Use the first four steps (Speak the Truth, Claim Territory, Brace for the Storm, and Ride the Wind) to find your way to a new sense of self. Then use Step Five to make certain that you do not lose yourself again.

Patrolling Borders After Finding Yourself

If you lost yourself in a relationship (marriage or otherwise) and have done the work of discovering who you are again, patrolling your borders is crucial. Even after building and repairing your fences, you are vulnerable. It's oh-so-easy to repeat the pattern.

My Story

After my first marriage I was very intentional about reclaiming and redefining myself. I had been so focused on being what I thought my husband wanted, and obsessed with his life, that I was distanced from my sense of self. So I set about becoming more independent and more me. I made a list of things I needed to do in order to rediscover who I was, checking them off as I did them. Here are some suggestions from my list:

- Go out to dinner by yourself.
- Take a trip alone.
- Go on a spiritual retreat.

- Take a class at your local community college.
- Go to the movies alone.
- Schedule a manicure or pedicure.
- Enroll in an exercise class (like aerobics, spinning, yoga, martial arts, or Pilates).
- Try out a new hobby (like golf, painting, volunteer work, tennis, or scrapbooking).
- Have a party.
- Get a massage.
- Redecorate a room, or your whole house!
- Make something grow: get a new houseplant, plant some flowers, make an herb garden, or grow your own tomatoes.
- Reconnect with old friends.
- Get to know some people in the same boat as you.

Try doing some things you might like! If you can't even remember what you like anymore, take a chance and try something new.

I did find myself, and I enjoyed the process. I certainly felt better. But as soon as I began a serious relationship, I forgot almost everything I had learned. As time went by my boundaries eroded. I focused on meeting my partner's needs and ignoring my own again. We traveled where he wanted, ate what he preferred, and spent our time together doing mostly what he wanted to do. If only I had been more diligent in checking my fences, I could have avoided the creeping resentment that soaked into me like syrup on pancakes. Of course, I became unhappy and dissatisfied in the relationship and eventually ended it.

I walk my property lines all the time now, and I'm sure it's part of why my marriage works so well. If my husband's agenda slips under my fence too often, or I find myself spending more time tending his fields than my own, I take action. It doesn't have to be much. Sometimes it simply means I leave him to his own devices and go out to dinner with girlfriends. Sometimes I take a trip without him. I might fix something I like for dinner, even if it is not one of his favorites. Every now and then I insist he go to a social event with me that he would rather avoid. Nothing earth-shattering, just little things, but it's little things that make up a relationship and little resentments that can tear one apart.

Patrolling Borders with Children

Wise parents who diligently set limits for their children early on are not as apt to have unruly teenagers. At about two years of age, toddlers challenge the structures around them: hence the adage "terrible twos." We could call them fence-busters. If all goes well, the little tyrants discover that they are no match for the firm, solid fences their parents have erected. When children learn that they are not stronger than the structures containing them, they are reassured and decide that the world is safe.

Fence-busting is revisited in adolescence. If you think your teenager acts just like a two-year-old, you're right! Once again your offspring challenge the limits, and once again, if all goes well, they find a solid structure. Teenagers aren't ready (developmentally) to be stronger than their parents. As much as they may push against them, when fences stand firm they feel safe.

Patrolling borders with twos and teens requires diligence. It's exhausting work: you have to spot every weakness in the fence and repair it before it becomes a problem.

Ashley's Story

Ashley's parents ran a tight ship. The household rules were spelled out in writing and posted on the refrigerator. Both parents were involved in school activities—Ashley's mom was on the PTA and her dad was an officer in the booster club. Ashley flourished within her parents' boundaries. At fourteen she was an honor student, an athlete, and a leader in her peer group.

The next year her parents went through a long and contentious divorce. The divorce process lingered like a chronic disease, and the parents became absorbed in their own pain and frustration. When it was finally over, their energy was invested in finding new partners. They didn't worry about Ashley. After all, she had always been an ideal child.

By age sixteen, Ashley had morphed into a stranger. Her grades dropped. She quit volleyball and swimming and started hanging out with kids who were in trouble. Isolating herself in her room, she became increasingly uncommunicative with her parents. She lied about her whereabouts. When her mother found drug paraphernalia in her backpack, she called Ashley's father and then called me. For the sake of their daughter, the parents agreed to see me together. I suggested they invite their significant others as well, which they did.

In the course of our session both parents acknowledged abandoning their heretofore well-defined limits with Ashley. They felt guilty about the divorce and thought giving her more freedom would be seen as evidence of their love for her. Unfortunately, it backfired.

As the four adults shared stories, it became clear that Ashley was lying and manipulating, using one parent against the other. The game was over. Her parents and their partners worked together to reestablish the old limits and formulate new ones.

This is just one example of how easy it is to lose control of children when parents forget, or fail, or choose not to patrol boundaries. I want to mention here that boundaries should and do change as children mature. The limits set for a twelve-year-old should not be the same as those for a fourteen-year-old. Patrolling boundaries gives parents the opportunity to evaluate and move fences as age and situations change.

Patrolling Borders with Parents

Once offspring successfully separate emotionally from their parents, adulthood begins. That's not to say adult children don't need a close relationship with their parents anymore, because they do. Nor does it mean that grown children do not value or esteem their parents. But it does mean that adult children should take responsibility for their own lives. Emotional fences, like real fences, are vulnerable to wear and tear, inclement weather, and blunt trauma. Adult children should patrol the emotional fences between themselves and their parents on a regular basis. Preventive maintenance may thwart a collapse and protect a relationship.

Gina's Story

Shortly after Gina married, she began complaining to her mother about her husband—just the little things that this man, whom Gina genuinely loved, did that annoyed her. The mother took this as an invitation to air her true feelings, and it did not take long for Gina's mother to tell her what she really thought of her choice for a mate. Mother and daughter were soon at odds. Mom became hypervigilant around her new son-in-law and was quick to criticize his slightest weakness. Gina defended the man she loved.

Gina made an oh-so-common but oh-so-dangerous mistake. Being close to her mother, she forgot that her mother would probably not make the greatest confidante. Women can, and do, complain bitterly about their husbands to their girlfriends; it's acceptable "girl talk," but it comes with clear boundaries. Girlfriends listen, commiserate, and support each other.

Mothers are a different story. Ever protective of their children, mothers are prone to react strongly to their daughter's (or son's) unhappiness. Gina failed to patrol her borders, and now her mother was well inside the heart of her personal space.

Mark and Sally's Story

Mark and Sally wanted to buy a house. Sally fell in love with a quaint bungalow, but they could not afford the down payment. Sally just knew this was the home for them, so she pressed Mark to ask his parents for a loan. His parents were glad to help the young couple financially, but Mark's father did not approve of their choice; he pressured "the kids" to buy his pick, a ranch-style house that neither Mark nor Sally were enthusiastic about.

Now the couple was caught between a rock and a hard place. They wanted the bungalow but knew they would feel guilty about taking money from Mark's father if they ignored his advice about which house to buy.

It is always good to patrol borders with parents, but it is especially crucial to do so before making major life transitions. Moving in together, getting married, making a major purchase, having a baby, changing a job, or taking a major trip are important life events, and they are personal. There is nothing wrong with discussing your plans with your parents and asking for their opinion and advice. There *is* something wrong with following your parents' advice when you do not want to because you are afraid you will hurt their feelings (in other words, feel guilty) if you don't.

Patrolling Borders at Work

Being a therapist is the perfect career for me in a number of ways. One of the things I appreciate most is that the territory comes with well-defined boundaries. Financial requirements, contact possibilities, and ethical mandates are etched in stone.

I explain the parameters to my clients right up front: I work a fifty-minute session for a given fee. If issues remain at the end of fifty minutes and my client wants to spend more time with me, he or she can make another appointment. Phone calls between sessions are free but are limited to ten minutes. The clock starts running after ten minutes and clients are charged for the time. I do not take calls at home except in the case of a serious crisis. My only relationship with my clients is a professional one; I do not socialize with them.

Being a college chaplain was a whole different story. I had already burned out of a couple of careers before I took on campus ministry, and I had learned a lot about claiming territory. However, I had not learned the importance of patrolling borders.

In campus ministry the territory was open range. There weren't any fences in sight. It was supposed to be a half-time position, but I could never quite find the cutoff point. Students walked into my office whenever they felt like it and stayed as long as they wanted. They called me at home whenever the mood struck. "TGIF" was no longer a declaration of freedom from work for me because weekend activities were part of the package. Do not get me wrong; it wasn't that I was unhappy in my position. I loved the students and loved my job, but it almost killed me. Since I had no delineated boundaries, my territory seemed endless and I felt responsible for all of it.

About three years into my bi-vocational adventure as a chaplain and a therapist, I realized that I had neither created nor patrolled boundaries. I decided something had to be done because I was drowning. So I surveyed my territory and marked boundaries.

I could not have done it alone. My husband knew all too well how my time and energy were being used. He was more than ready to help me build fences. For those of us fueled by the guilt of never doing enough or being enough, the input of someone close to us is invaluable.

I established office hours and curtailed weekend projects and activities. I got caller I.D. and didn't *always* answer my phone. I created an advisory board and delegated responsibilities. I appointed student leaders. The next four years were much better; I was happier and more effective in both my careers. The experience taught me to be diligent in claiming territory and patrolling the borders.

There are plenty of jobs besides ministry that come without boundaries. Millions of salaried workers do not know the meaning of the forty-hour workweek. Unfortunately, it's not always possible to establish healthy boundaries if management has other ideas.

In my community most medical doctors are employed by two huge hospital systems. Gone are the days of the intimate doctor-patient relationship that characterized medical practice in the past. Medicine is big business, and profit margin is the bottom line. My clients who are physicians are pushed to the limit. It's all about productivity; the more patients they see in a day, the better. See more patients, do more surgery, take more calls, make more rounds. Something has to give, and sometimes it is the doctor's health. Slowly, one by one, medical doctors are leaving the system and fighting non-competition clauses in their contracts in order to establish their own practices. I'm not saying this is the answer to the medical care crisis in the United States, but I am saying that jobs without boundaries are not good for people.

Border Patrol Techniques

The following is a list of ideas that may be helpful to you when it is time to patrol your borders:

• **Use self-talk.** Having an honest conversation with yourself can be illuminating. If you find yourself falling back into old habits, ask yourself if guilt is your motivation. Remember that taking good care of yourself is a primary goal. Ask yourself if you are enjoying life. Do you set aside time to have fun? Do you play? Are you spending time with friends?

• **Call on angels.** Nurture your spiritual life. Read a book that will help you focus on the mystery of God's presence in your life today. Attend worship services that remind you who you are and whom you serve. Participate in a spiritual study group. Pray.

- **Revisit the scene of the crime.** Revisit the way things were before you decided to exit the guilt trap. Look through photo albums and read old letters or e-mails. Think about how you felt then.

- **Write in your journal.** Write about your resolve to maintain the progress you have made. List the ways in which you feel better, freer, healthier, and more effective without toxic guilt.

- **Make an appointment with your therapist, spiritual director, mentor, or close friend.** Talk about the challenges of remaining free of toxic guilt. Confess setbacks and explore how you could have managed things better. Strategize about plans for the future.

- **Monitor your physical health.** Be sure you are eating well and exercising on a regular basis. If you feel tired and your energy level seems low, find out why. How are your weight and blood pressure? Are you sleeping well?

- **Ask, "What would this person say?"** If you are contemplating doing something that you really do not want to do but think you should, ask yourself what someone you respect and trust would say about that behavior.

- **Take time out.** Practice meditation, walk a labyrinth, go on a retreat (spiritual or otherwise), or take a vacation.

The High Cost of Failure

Failing to patrol borders is emotionally expensive. Do not forget the power of the familiar. If you are a rescuer, remember that rescuers return to their roots in a heartbeat. Those who would abuse your compassionate nature will head straight for your territory when they detect a boundary in disrepair. It is especially disheartening to build good emotional fences and experience inherent freedom from guilt only to find yourself sliding back to square one. That is exactly what happened to my husband and me.

My Story

We were at odds about our social life. Although I am more interested in cultivating and nurturing family relationships and couple friends than he is, we both tend to accommodate the desires of others instead of doing what we want to do, which is usually to be alone. If friends call with an invitation to get together, we agree whether we want to or not. We are both afraid that we would hurt our friends' feelings if we say no, so we acquiesce to avoid feeling guilty.

After numerous haphazard attempts to find a reasonable solution to our dilemma, we sat down together one night to address the situation formally (Step One, Speak the Truth). Finally, we negotiated a settlement that met both our needs (Step Two, Claim Territory). The solution was that on Friday nights we stay home; we do not invite friends in, and we do not go out. We do not answer the phone, either. Saturday nights we are open to socializing with family or friends. My husband's need for alone time was met, and my need for socialization was satisfied. It was a good plan.

When we notified friends and family of our plan, we got some snickers and raised eyebrows in response (Step Three, Brace for the Storm). There was an initial flurry of Friday night phone calls, which we did not answer, knowing it was just the people we love testing the system. We knew we were not being insensitive or uncaring; it was simply a boundary. We did not feel guilty when we met resistance because we had built a sensible plan to meet important needs (Step Four, Ride the Wind).

At first we stuck to our guns diligently, but over time we became negligent. Slowly but surely Friday night events crept in and we made exceptions, usually to please others. Finally our Friday night ritual disappeared altogether. My husband became irritable and out-of-sorts; I was anxious and on edge.

One Friday night when we were home alone, we had a serious conversation about our relationship. Realizing what had happened, we recommitted to our plan (Step Five, Patrol Borders). We could not blame others for trespassing on our territory; we were the ones who failed to patrol our borders and check our fences.

I hope you are now well on your way to deciding to live life fully and joyfully, on your own terms, and free from toxic guilt. I hope you understand and even like yourself better than you did when you picked up this book. And I hope you feel courageous. Remember that life is a journey, but the journey does not have to be a guilt trip. The going will not always be smooth, but you do have the right to make your own decisions and act on them, in good times and bad.

Celebrate your caring, compassionate spirit—protect it and treat it well. Do not despair when you manage to navigate your way through rough waters only to find another storm looming ahead; celebrate the fact that you are the captain of your ship. When toxic guilt threatens to smash your vessel on the rocks and you feel fear taking over, recall the five steps to freedom and take action.

1. **Speak the truth.** The truth will set you free.
2. **Claim territory.** You have the right to do what you want to do.
3. **Brace for the storm.** Other people will not like it when you stop accommodating them.
4. **Ride the wind.** Let go of the illusion of control; what is, is.
5. **Patrol borders.** Beware of old behavior patterns. Repair and maintain your fences.

Index